# Mometrix

Product ID: PrIIECEd5025 2/2

# TEST PREPARATION

# Praxis II
## Early Childhood Education (5025) Exam Secrets Study Guide
### Part 2 of 2

Praxis II Test Review for the
Praxis II: Subject Assessments

# Mometrix®
## PREP THAT EMPOWERS

# **FREE** Study Skills Videos/DVD Offer

Dear Customer,

Thank you for your purchase from Mometrix! We consider it an honor and a privilege that you have purchased our product and we want to ensure your satisfaction.

As a way of showing our appreciation and to help us better serve you, we have developed Study Skills Videos that we would like to give you for <u>FREE</u>. These videos cover our *best practices* for getting ready for your exam, from how to use our study materials to how to best prepare for the day of the test.

All that we ask is that you email us with feedback that would describe your experience so far with our product. Good, bad, or indifferent, we want to know what you think!

To get your FREE Study Skills Videos, you can use the **QR code** below, or send us an **email** at <u>studyvideos@mometrix.com</u> with *FREE VIDEOS* in the subject line and the following information in the body of the email:

- The name of the product you purchased.
- Your product rating on a scale of 1-5, with 5 being the highest rating.
- Your feedback. It can be long, short, or anything in between. We just want to know your impressions and experience so far with our product. (Good feedback might include how our study material met your needs and ways we might be able to make it even better. You could highlight features that you found helpful or features that you think we should add.)

If you have any questions or concerns, please don't hesitate to contact me directly.

Thanks again!

Sincerely,

Jay Willis
Vice President
<u>jay.willis@mometrix.com</u>
1-800-673-8175

# Praxis II

## Early Childhood Education (5025) Exam Secrets Study Guide

Part 2 of 2

# DEAR FUTURE EXAM SUCCESS STORY

First of all, **THANK YOU** for purchasing Mometrix study materials!

Second, congratulations! You are one of the few determined test-takers who are committed to doing whatever it takes to excel on your exam. **You have come to the right place.** We developed these study materials with one goal in mind: to deliver you the information you need in a format that's concise and easy to use.

In addition to optimizing your guide for the content of the test, we've outlined our recommended steps for breaking down the preparation process into small, attainable goals so you can make sure you stay on track.

We've also analyzed the entire test-taking process, identifying the most common pitfalls and showing how you can overcome them and be ready for any curveball the test throws you.

Standardized testing is one of the biggest obstacles on your road to success, which only increases the importance of doing well in the high-pressure, high-stakes environment of test day. Your results on this test could have a significant impact on your future, and this guide provides the information and practical advice to help you achieve your full potential on test day.

### Your success is our success

**We would love to hear from you!** If you would like to share the story of your exam success or if you have any questions or comments in regard to our products, please contact us at **800-673-8175** or **support@mometrix.com**.

Thanks again for your business and we wish you continued success!

Sincerely,
The Mometrix Test Preparation Team

---

**Need more help? Check out our flashcards at:**
**http://MometrixFlashcards.com/PraxisII**

---

# TABLE OF CONTENTS

# Mathematics

## Emergent Mathematics

### ASSESSING SKILLS EXAMPLE

A kindergarten teacher arranges colored beads in the following order: red, blue, yellow, red, blue. She asks her students which bead should come next. Discuss and explain the importance of the skill being assessed.

The kindergarten teacher is assessing the student's ability to recognize and extend a pattern. If the student has mastered this skill, he or she will state that the next color in the pattern is yellow. Understanding patterns is an important prerequisite skill for the development of mathematics for several reasons. It helps students to build memory, use logic, make educated guesses, and develop critical thinking skills. In addition, patterns are the first step in understanding the language of algebra. To help students develop their mastery of patterns, the teacher can provide a variety of learning experiences. For instance, the teacher can find a pattern in the classroom, such as the stripes on someone's shirt, and point out the pattern of colors. Another great way to practice patterns is to get the students moving. Have them jump, touch their heads, then clap their hands in a repeated pattern. Teachers can easily incorporate patterns across other disciplines, such as different sounds in music or colored beads for an art project. Any and all exposure with identifying and extending patterns will help to strengthen critical thinking skills necessary for lifelong learners.

### DETERMINING THE NEXT SHAPE IN A SEQUENCE EXAMPLE

A fifth-grade teacher draws the following set of figures on the board: a triangle, a rectangle, and a pentagon. Determine the next shape of the sequence. Explain your reasoning.

The next shape of the sequence is a hexagon. To recognize a pattern, we must analyze the attributes of each term already included in the sequence. Here, we have a three-sided polygon, a four-sided polygon, and finally a five-sided polygon. Once we have identified the key attribute of each term (in this case, the number of sides on each polygon), we can determine how those attributes relate to one another. The numbers 3, 4, and 5 are counting numbers, which means the next number in our pattern must be 6. From here, we must connect our knowledge of geometry. Since a six-sided polygon is called a hexagon, we can infer that the next term in the pattern is a hexagon. Teachers can extend the practice of patterns by creating learning experiences that match the ability level of the learner. A higher-level numerical pattern might look like "1, 3, 4, 7, 11." Here, the student would have to realize that each term is the sum of the two prior terms (1 + 3 = 4, 3 + 4 = 7, and so on). Here, the next term in the sequence would be the sum of 7 and 11, which is 18.

### ONE-TO-ONE CORRESPONDENCE EXAMPLE

A student is counting objects incorrectly. Identify and discuss the skill the student is struggling to master. List ways the teacher can help the student improve this skill.

1

Although the student may have memorized the order of counting numbers, he/she is struggling to master one-to-one correspondence. One-to-one correspondence is the skill in which each item in a set is counted exactly one time. This ensures that the total number of objects is accurately represented as the whole. When a student is struggling with one-to-one correspondence, he/she will make errors when trying to determine the total number of items in a set. The student may be skipping objects that have not yet been counted, or counting the same object more than once. To improve one-to-one-correspondence, the teacher should explain to the student that each object must have exactly one "name," which corresponds with its counting number. In addition, the teacher should start by providing the student with only two or three objects to count at a time. As the student consistently counts the objects correctly, the teacher can add more objects to the group, thus strengthening the student's mastery of one-to-one correspondence.

## ATTRIBUTE

In mathematics, the term "attribute" refers to a characteristic or property of an object or shape. Examples of attributes can include many things, such as the shape of an object or the number of sides a shape consists of. Attributes can go on to describe how the sides of a shape relate to one another, or the different types of angles enclosed in a shape. In addition, attributes can be used to describe the color, size, or orientation of a shape.

## ATTRIBUTES OF RECTANGLES AND TRAPEZOIDS

While comparing and contrasting rectangles and trapezoids, it is important to note that both rectangles and trapezoids are considered polygons, and both consist of four sides. Rectangles have two sets of equivalent sides, both of which are parallel to each other. Trapezoids, by definition, have only one set of parallel sides. In addition, rectangles include four right angles, while trapezoids do not.

## ATTRIBUTE EXAMPLE

A child is given a bucket full of triangles, squares, and circles randomly colored blue, green, and red. Give two different attributes the student may use to group the shapes.

In this example, the student is being assessed on his or her ability to classify objects by a defining characteristic. Here, the student may choose to classify the objects by shape *or* color. Both options would allow the student to group the objects based on a defining attribute. Should the student choose to group the objects by shape, he or she would group all the triangles, squares, and circles into separate piles, regardless of color. On the other hand, if the student chooses to sort the objects by color, he or she would create groups of blue, green, and red objects, regardless of shape. The ability to classify objects is an important math skill because it forces students to compare and contrast objects carefully, following a specific set of rules. It also helps to develop real-world skills, such as logical ways to organize toys or clothes. Teachers can provide opportunities to practice classification in everyday classroom activities such as organizing the art supplies or setting up the classroom library.

## SUBITIZING

Subitizing is the ability to recognize an amount without counting each object individually. A student that has mastered this skill can roll a die and instantly know what they've rolled, without counting the dots. He or she might also look at a full dinner table and instantly know that six people are seated, without counting each individual person. Subitizing is an important math skill because it allows students to quickly determine totals, while saving their mental energy to focus on more complex problems. It also helps students to master addition and subtraction facts more easily, since they have already developed strategies for mentally compensating for more or less of a specific amount. Furthermore, these students often develop more practical counting strategies, such as counting by twos in order to quickly determine the number of objects in a large group.

> **Review Video: Addition, Subtraction, Multiplication, and Division**
> Visit mometrix.com/academy and enter code: 208095

## SUBITIZING EXAMPLE

A child is rolling a dice. Each time, he must count the dots to determine the number he has rolled. Identify the skill the student is struggling to master and discuss ways the teacher can help the student to develop this skill.

> The student is struggling with subitizing, or in other words, the ability to instantly determine an amount without counting each individual object. Students with a strong grasp of subitizing are able to recognize patterns, usually in the form of dots, and use quick compensation strategies to determine the total. For example, a student may instantly recognize that four dots on a dice represents '4' and use that skill to quickly realize the '4' pattern plus an extra dot in the middle is used to represent '5' on a die. In order to help develop the skill of subitizing the teacher can provide games involving dice or dominoes to strengthen number sense. In addition, teachers can provide students with matching games in which the students race to match the numeric representations of numbers to the visual representations. For example, students flip over a card with seven dots and race one another to find the card with the number '7' as its match.

## CONSERVATION OF NUMBER EXAMPLE

A child is asked to compare two sets of identical objects. Each set has the objects arranged in a different way. The child asserts that the first set contains more objects than the second set. Identify and discuss the skill that this student has not yet mastered.

> The student has not yet mastered the conservation of number concept. This concept refers to a student's ability to recognize that the total number of objects in a group remains the same, regardless of how those objects are arranged. To strengthen this skill, teachers can provide students with an equal number of different colored counters and allow the students to arrange each set in any way they would like. For example, a student may be given five red counters and five yellow counters. The student may choose to arrange the red counters in a straight line, close together, while the yellow counters are arranged to create a big circle. The teacher should then ask the student which arrangement contains the greater number of counters. If the student chooses one group over the other, the teacher should ask questions such as, "Did you receive any extra counters to create that arrangement?" or "Did you forget to use any of your counters?" The teacher should use the student's responses to guide the revelation that the number of objects in a set does not change based on the way those objects are arranged.

## SEQUENCE EXAMPLE

A student is asked to fill in the blanks for the following pattern: 10, 20, 30, ___, ___, 60. Identify the skill being assessed and discuss strategies for helping the student successfully complete the pattern.

> The student is being assessed on her ability to sequence. In mathematics, sequencing is similar to recognizing and extending patterns. Here, the student must first realize that each term is ten more than the term before it. In other words, the terms in the sequence can be determined by simply counting by tens. The student can check the pattern by inserting 40 and 50 in the blanks. Since ten more than 50 is 60, and 60 is the next given term, the student can be sure he/she has sequenced correctly. Teachers can help students to develop the skill of sequencing by providing students with a 100 number board and various colored pencils. Students can explore different sequences by shading all the numbers in various patterns such as counting by twos, fives, or tens. As students develop this skill they will improve their number sense, thus making more challenging math problems easier to calculate and understand.

## POSITION AND PROXIMITY

The term "position" refers to an object's location in relationship to something else. For example, the paper is on the desk, or the pencil is under the chair. The term "proximity" is used to describe the relative distance an object is located from another object. For example, the movie theater is near the school, but far from the park. The ability to use words to describe the position or proximity of objects is an important pre-math skill because it helps to develop spatial reasoning and mathematical language. This type of reasoning will be especially helpful as students begin to learn geometry and measurement. Teachers can help to develop these skills at an early age by creating scavenger hunts in which the students must follow clues that use words such as *on*, *under*, *behind*, *above*, etc. to describe the locations of future clues. As students search for clues they are learning the definitions of important words, while truly strengthening their spatial reasoning skills.

## WORDS DESCRIBING POSITION OR PROXIMITY

There are many words that can be used to describe position or proximity in mathematics. Some of these words include (but are not limited to) *up*, *down*, *above*, *below*, *near*, *far*, *over*, *under*, *in front of*, *behind*, *left*, or *right*. Teachers can help students to practice these words in many ways. One way is to invite students to bring in a photograph from home. Then, have each student describe his or her photo using words to describe the location of the objects (or people) in the photograph in relation to one another. For example, the student may say, "My dad is standing behind my mom," or "The flower vase is on top of the table." Another way to practice these words is to show students a picture with a lot of detail and ask the students to answer questions about the scene. For example, "Is the bear in front of or behind the tree?"

## IMPORTANCE OF REPRESENTING NUMBERS IN VARIOUS WAYS

It is important that students are taught to represent numbers in various ways because it strengthens the students' overall number sense. Number sense refers to the conceptual understanding of how numbers are organized, what they represent, and how they relate to one another. Students with strong number sense are able to work more fluently with numbers, have good estimation skills, and can apply their knowledge of numbers to solve more complex problems. Teachers can help students to develop their number sense by providing opportunities to express numbers in several ways. For example, the number 52 can be broken down by place value and expressed in expanded form as 50 + 2. For younger students, teachers can provide manipulatives such as base-ten blocks to create five groups of tens and two groups of ones. Other ideas for

4

expressing numbers in various ways include tally charts, drawings, written words, or sums of numbers.

## WAYS TO REPRESENT THE NUMBER 37

A student can represent the number 37 in several different ways. Using place value, the student can break apart the number into separate pieces. This would force the student to think of the '3' as '30'(or three tens) and the '7' as simply seven ones. Students can use this knowledge to write 37 in expanded form as 30 + 7. Students might also choose to use this thought process to draw a visual representation of 30 + 7 by drawing three groups of tens along with seven groups of ones. In addition, students can represent 37 as the words "thirty-seven" or use tally charts to draw seven bundles (each containing five tallies) and two individual tallies. The student might also choose to represent 37 by drawing a visual representation of objects, or as the sum of other compatible numbers.

## RELATIONSHIP BETWEEN COUNTING AND CARDINALITY

The principles of counting and cardinality are closely related. When counting, a student must understand and demonstrate one-to-one correspondence. Once that is mastered, the student can move on to the concept of cardinality. Cardinality is the measure of elements in a set. For example, when given a set of ten objects a student can demonstrate the ability to count the objects by pointing at each object one at a time, while assigning each object a number in the appropriate order. If the student reaches the tenth object and then asserts that there are ten objects in the group, that student has demonstrated an understanding of the cardinality principle. In other words, the ability to count comes *before* the concept of cardinality. A student must first count the objects before he or she can make the connection that the last number counted represents the total number of objects in the set.

# Numbers and Operations

## COMPARING WHOLE NUMBERS EXAMPLE

A student is struggling to compare whole numbers that include an equal number of digits. Develop a strategy that the student can use to compare these numbers effectively.

> When comparing whole numbers containing an equal number of digits, students can decide which number has the greater value by comparing the digits in the far left place value of each number. For example, when comparing 495 to 382, the student can look at the 4 and the 3 to decide which number has the greater value. Since the 4 represents 400, and the 3 represents 300, the student can conclude that 495 is greater than 382 since the hundreds place is the greatest place value represented and 400 is always greater than 300. Students can modify this strategy when dealing with digits of equal value. Let's say a student was to compare 724 to 789. When they look to the far left they have 7's in the hundreds place of each number. Since 700 is equivalent to 700, they will have to compare the digits in the next place value. Here, those numbers are 2 and 8. Since the 2 represents 20 and the 8 represents 80, the student can conclude that 724 is less than 789 since 20 is less than 80.

## DETERMINING GREATER VALUE EXAMPLE

Consider the numbers 904 and 940. Determine which number has the greater value and explain your reasoning.

When comparing two whole numbers with an equivalent number of digits we can decide which has the greater value by comparing the digit in their greatest place value. The greatest place-value of a number is the place value to the far left of that number. Here, we're comparing the hundreds place. Since both numbers have a 9 in the hundreds place, we must move on to the next biggest place value. In other words, we must compare the digits one place value to the right of our largest place value. In this example, we're now comparing the tens place. Since 0 is less than 4, we can conclude that 904 is less than 940. This is true because although both numbers have nine hundreds, 904 does not have any tens, while 940 has four tens. That means 940 has a greater value than 904.

## ORDERING NUMBERS FROM LEAST TO GREATEST EXAMPLE

Order the following set of numbers from least to greatest. {67,829; 76,928; 103,849; 103,894; 1,039}. Explain your reasoning.

From least to greatest the numbers are 1,039; 67,829; 76,928; 103,849; 103,894. Since we're working with whole numbers (all of which have first digits greater than zero), we can count the number of digits to identify 1,039 as having the smallest value. Next, we must compare 67,829 and 76,928. The quickest way to compare two numbers with the same number of digits is to compare the digit in their greatest place value (the digit to the far left). Here, we're comparing the ten-thousands place. Since 6 is less than 7, we know that 67,829 is less than 76,928. Finally, we can compare our last subset, 103,849 and 103,894. We notice that both numbers start with a 1, making their hundred-thousands place value equivalent. When this happens, we must continue moving over one place value to the right until we find a place value with digits that are not identical. In this case, the greatest non-equivalent place value is the tens place. Since 4 is less than 9, we know that 103,849 is less than 103,894. In summary, our set from least to greatest is 1,039; 67,829; 76,928; 103,849; 103,894.

## DECOMPOSING A NUMBER

Decomposing a number is a way to truly examine the value of that number. Most often, we use decomposition to break a multi-digit number into a numerical expression that showcases that number as the sum of its parts. Let's use 726 as an example. To decompose this number we traditionally start with the number in the greatest place value. In this case, we'll start with the 7. Since the 7 is in the hundreds place value, we know its value is 700. We'll use that later on as the first addend of our number sentence. Next, we move on to the tens place value, where we find a 2. That makes our 2 truly worth 20. We'll use 20 as the second addend of our number sentence. Finally, we can move on to our final digit, the 6. The 6 is in the ones place, making its value simply 6 (our final addend). Now that we've determined the value of each digit, we can decompose 726 to create the number sentence 700 + 20 + 6. Decomposition of a number is useful when comparing the values of different numbers or when trying to mentally calculate larger numbers.

## DECOMPOSING A NUMBER EXAMPLES

Jaxen decomposes the number 892 as 80 + 90 + 2. Identify and correct his mistake.

Jaxen's decomposition is incorrect due to a place value error. The 8 in 892 is in the hundreds place, making its value 800, not 80. The correct way to decompose 892 is 800 + 90 + 2. A quick trick for writing the value of each place value is to keep the digit you are focusing on the same, while replacing all place values to the right with zeros. For example, with 892, Jaxen was correct to start with the 8 since it is the digit to the far left (the greatest place value). However, to determine the 8's true value, he could count how many digits are in the number 892 to the right of 8. Since there are two digits to the right of the 8 (9 and 2), he could simply replace them with two zeros to determine that the 8 is worth 800, not 80.

Determine what number has been decomposed to create the number sentence 300 + 9. Explain your reasoning.

> The number sentence 300 + 9 represents the value 309. We can determine this by simply adding 300 and 9. We can check that we are right by working backwards to decompose 309. Since our greatest place value is the hundreds place, we know the 3 is worth 300. When we move to our next place value, the tens, we find a zero. Since zero tens is worth zero, we do not have to include it in our number sentence. Finally, we move on to the ones place, which contains a 9. Any digit in the ones place simply retains its value, meaning the 9 in the ones place has a value of 9. When we piece it back together we know that we can decompose 309 to 300 + 9, proving our original answer correct.

## PLACE VALUE EXAMPLES

List the names of each place value, from left to right, from the thousands place to the thousandths place.

> From left to right, the place values are: thousands, hundreds, tens, ones, tenths, hundredths, thousandths. A trick for remembering the place values when transitioning from whole number to decimal place values is to think of them as a mirror image of each other, with the exception of the ones place. If we remember that there is only *one* ones place, we can think of the place values to the right of the decimal point as a mirror image of the place values to the left of the decimal place, only in reverse order. We must remember to omit the ones place since it is "one of a kind." By adding "-th" to the end of every other place value in reverse (like a mirror) we can list the decimal place values. For example, tens become tenths, hundreds become hundredths and thousands become thousandths.

> **Review Video: Number Place Value**
> Visit mometrix.com/academy and enter code: 205433

A number has the digit "4" two place values to the right of the decimal point. Name the place value of the digit and explain its value.

> The value of the 4 is four hundredths, or .04. The first step to identifying its value is to determine which place value is two places to the right of the decimal point. Any digit positioned two place values to the right of the decimal point is in the hundredths place, making its value one-hundredth of a whole. Here, a 4 in the hundredths place is worth four hundredths. An easy way to make sense of hundredths is to think of money. There are one hundred cents in every dollar, making each cent worth one one-hundredth of a dollar. Four hundredths has the same value as four cents, since the numbers are representing values that are one-hundredths of a whole.

## DETERMINING GREATER VALUE EXAMPLES

Consider the number 54.392. Determine whether the "4" or the "3" has a greater value. Explain your reasoning.

> When comparing numbers, the non-zero digit to the left always has a greater value than the digit to the right. Since the 4 is to the left of the 3, its value must be greater. Furthermore, the 4 is to the left of the decimal point, making it a whole number, while the 3 is to the right of the decimal point, making it worth less than a whole. In other words, the 3 is worth only *part* of a whole. Any non-zero whole number will always have a greater value than a number representing less than a whole. Another strategy for comparing these values is to think of it as money. The 4 is in the ones place, making it worth $4.00, while the 3 is in the tenths place, making its value $0.30. Any way we look at it, the 4 in the ones place is greater than the 3 in the tenths place.

Cooper believes that every digit has a value ten times greater than the digit to its left. Explain and correct his error.

> Cooper is correct in identifying our number system as a base-ten system, meaning our values increase and decrease by tens as we move left and right. However, Cooper is incorrect in his direction. To correct his error, Cooper should state that every digit has a value ten times greater than the digit to its *right*. For example, in the number 77, the 7 to the left is in the tens place, making its value 70. The 7 to the right is in the ones place, making its value 7. The place value to the left, 70, has a value ten times greater than the digit to its *right*, the 7.

## COMPARING THE VALUES OF NUMBERS EXAMPLE

Consider the number 0.44. Compare the value of the "4" in the tenths place to the value of the "4" in the hundredths place.

> Our number system is a base-ten number system, meaning every digit has a value ten times greater than the digit to its right. In this example, the 4 in the tenths place has a value ten times greater than the 4 in the hundredths place. When we write each digit as its true value, we can write the 4 in the tenths place as 0.4 and the 4 in the hundredths place as having a value of 0.04. When comparing decimals, it helps to think of the values as money. For example, 0.4 is the same as four tenths of a dollar, or 0.40, or 40 cents. Meanwhile, 0.04 is the equivalent of four hundredths of a dollar, or 4 cents. We know that 40 cents is worth ten times as much as 4 cents, so the 4 in the tenths place is worth tens times more than the 4 in the hundredths place.

## ROUNDING NUMBERS TO A SPECIFIC PLACE VALUE

When rounding numbers to specific place values we use the digit to the right of that place value to determine whether to "round up" or remain the same. If the number to the right is 5 or above, we increase the digit in the place value we're rounding by one whole and replace all place values to the right of that digit with zeros. All digits to the left of the place value we're rounding remain the same. If the digit to the right of the place value we're rounding is less than 5, we keep the digit in the place value we're rounding exactly the same and replace all digits to the right of that number with zeros. For example, when rounding 824 to the nearest hundred, we must identify the digit in the hundreds place, the 8. Next, we look at the digit to the right of the 8. The number to the right of the 8 is 2.

Since 2 is less than 5, the 8 remains the same and we replace all digits to the right of the 8 with zeros. That number 824 rounded to the nearest hundred is 800.

## ROUNDING NUMBER EXAMPLES

Round the number 65.718 to the nearest whole number. Explain your process.

> In order to round 65.718 to the nearest whole number, we must first recognize that 65 represents 65 wholes, while 718 represents part of a whole. Here, we need to determine if 65 should remain 65, or if we should increase it to 66. To make that decision, we look at the digit to the right of our whole number. In this example, the digit to the immediate right of our whole number is the 7 in the tenths place. Since 7 is greater than 5, we need to increase our whole number by one whole. That increases 65 wholes to 66 wholes. The number 65.718 rounded to the nearest whole number is simply 66.

Round the number 9.998 to the nearest tenth. Explain why this specific problem may be tricky for students and how you would assist them.

> To round 9.998 to the nearest tenth, we first identify the tenths place. Here, the 9 to the immediate right of the decimal point is in the tenths place. To determine whether or not to round up, we look at the digit to its right. Here, that digit is another 9. Since 9 is greater than 5, we must round the 9 in our tenths place up. This can be tricky because 9 cannot be increased to 10 since the number 10 takes up two place values and we can only fill the tenths place with one digit. When this happens, we must carry the extra digit to the left. A good strategy to help students who may struggle with this is to have them think of this as carrying the extra digit as we do when we're adding multi-digit numbers and have a sum greater than 9. After bringing the extra digit to the left, we find ourselves in the ones place, turning the 9 wholes into 10 wholes. That makes 9.998 rounded to the nearest tenth 10.0. Since we're rounding to the tenths place, it's helpful that we represent the tenths place as 10.0 and not just 10.

## EXPANDED FORM VS. STANDARD FORM

Standard form is the way in which we typically represent numbers. For example, the numbers 48 and 83,957 are both written in standard form. Expanded form is when we break apart a number in standard form and write it as a number sentence representing the sum of each digit's true value. For example, to write 48 in expanded form we must first determine that the 4 in the tens place really represents 40, while the 8 in the ones place represents 8. We can write 48 in expanded form as 40 + 8. Similarly, we would break apart the value of each digit in 83,957 to write it in expanded form as 80,000 + 3,000 + 900 + 50 + 7.

## EXPANDED FORM EXAMPLES

Write the number 4,938 in expanded form. Explain your process.

> The number 4,938 written in expanded form is 4,000 + 900 + 30 + 8. To start, we must determine the value of each digit, based on its place value. Since the 4 is in the thousands place, its value is 4,000. Similarly, the 9 is in the hundreds place, making its value 900. Since the 3 is in the tens place, we know its value is 30. Finally, we arrive at the 8 in the ones place, which is simply worth 8. To write our number in expanded form we must create a numerical expression combining these values. This is how we arrive at our expanded form of 4,000 + 900 + 30 + 8.

9

Write the number 28.603 in expanded form. Explain your process.

The number 28.603 written in expanded form is 20 + 8 + 0.6 + 0.003. Writing decimals in expanded form is similar to writing whole numbers in expanded form. We just have to be extra careful to represent each digit as its true value. Here, we can start by breaking our whole number, 28, into 20 + 8. Next, we have to break apart the decimal portion of our number. The 6 is in the tenths place, making its value 0.6. The zero in the hundredths place is worth zero, so we do not have to include it in our expanded form. Finally, the 3 in the thousandths place can be represented as the value 0.003. When we write all of our values as a numeric expression we have our expanded form of 20 + 8 + 0.6 + 0.003.

## MENTALLY MULTIPLYING EXAMPLES

Discuss how to use the decomposition of numbers to mentally multiply 42 by 3.

We can use the strategy of decomposing numbers to mentally calculate larger numbers. In this process, we must think of larger numbers in expanded form, then calculate each part of that expanded form separately. To find the product of 42 and 3, we must first expand 42 to 40 + 2. Then, we multiply each term in the expression by 3 and find the sum of those products. To start, we can mentally find the product of 40 and 3, which is 120. Then, we must find the product of 2 times 3, which is 6. Finally, we can add 120 and 6 to find our final answer of 126. The product of 42 and 3 is 126.

Explain how you can use the compensation strategy to mentally multiply 198 by 3.

The compensation strategy can be used to calculate numbers that are close to compatible numbers. Side note: compatible numbers are numbers that we can easily calculate mentally. When trying to multiply 198 by 3, we might notice that 198 is close to 200, and 200 times 3 is an easy problem to calculate. If we multiply 200 times 3, we can then use the compensation strategy to adjust our answer to reflect the product of 198 times 3. First, we must calculate our compatible numbers, 200 and 3, which gives us 600. Then, we need to determine how much higher our estimate is than our actual product. Since 200 is 2 more than 198 we must multiply 2 by 3 (our other factor). The product of 2 times 3 is 6. This tells us that our estimate, 600, is 6 more than what our actual product should be. Finally, we compensate. Since 600 − 6 = 594, we know that 198 times 3 is 594.

Josie wants to mentally multiply 299 by 4. Determine whether the decomposition or compensation strategy would prove more expedient for Josie. Explain your reasoning.

To mentally multiply 299 by 4, Josie should use the compensation strategy. This is a better strategy for Josie because 299 is very close to 300 and 300 times 4 is easy to calculate. To start, Josie knows that 300 times 4 is 1,200. Next, Josie must calculate 1 times 4, since 299 is only one number less than 300. The product of 1 and 4 is 4, so Josie knows that her estimate of 1,200 is four more than the product of 299 times 4. Four less than 1,200 is 1,196, making the product of 299 and 4 equivalent to 1,196. Had Josie chosen the decomposition strategy, she would have had to mentally multiply 200 by 4, 90 by 4, and 9 by 4. This would have given her the products 800, 360, and 36, which aren't necessarily easy numbers to add together mentally.

## APPLYING ASSOCIATIVE AND COMMUTATIVE PROPERTIES

Using the associative and commutative properties helps us to reorder numerical expressions in ways that help us better organize data and mentally compute expressions. Let's use the example of (89 + 12) + 8. Finding the sum of 89 and 12 can get tricky, however using the associative property, we can slide the parentheses around 12 + 8, to mentally calculate a sum of 20. Once we know that two of the numbers have a sum of 20, we can easily calculate 20 + 89 = 109. The commutative property has the same advantages. Consider the expression 25 × 7 × 4. Finding this product mentally would be easier if we moved compatible numbers closer together. Here, 25 and 4 are compatible because they easily multiply to get a product of 100. We can use the commutative property to re-think this mentally as 25 × 4 × 7. Since 25 times 4 is 100, and 100 times 7 is 700, we know our product is 700.

## INCLUDED OPERATIONS WHEN APPLYING THE ASSOCIATIVE PROPERTY

We can apply the associative property to expressions containing only addition *or* only multiplication symbols. We cannot apply the associative property for subtraction, division, or any combination of operations. This is true because addition and multiplication problems are commutative, meaning that we can change the order in which things are combined or multiplied without affecting the sum or product. By applying the associative property and moving the parentheses, we are essentially affecting the order in which numbers are summed or multiplied. Consider the expression (35 + 48) + 2. The sum of these numbers remains the same, regardless of the order in which we add the terms. It's easier to mentally add 48 and 2 than it is to add 35 and 48. Using the associative property, we can slide the parentheses to add 48 and 2 to get 50, and then add 35 + 50 for a final sum of 85. If there were a subtraction or division sign in the problem, moving the order of the terms would affect our answer.

## REWRITING EXPRESSIONS EXAMPLE

Rewrite the expression 18 + 17 + 2 using the commutative property. Explain your process.

> Using the commutative property, we can rewrite this number sentence in an effort to move compatible numbers closer together. Here, our compatible numbers are 18 and 2, since they easily combine to make 20. If we rewrite the number sentence as 18 + 2 + 17, or 2 + 18 + 17, we can quickly compute that 18 and 2 make 20, then add 20 + 17 to find our total sum of 37. Using the commutative property and compatible numbers helps us to mentally calculate sums or products that otherwise might prove too challenging.

## USING NUMBER LINES TO REPRESENT THE MULTIPLICATION OR DIVISION OF WHOLE NUMBERS

Students can use number lines to visually see the multiplication or division of whole numbers. To multiply, students can use a number line to visually skip count to arrive at the product of two numbers. For instance, if a student wants to multiply 4 times 3, he or she can start at zero, drawing arrows that skip count by 4s. Since the problem is 4 times 3, they need to continue skip counting three times, until they arrive at their product, 12. Similarly, students can use number lines to visualize division. If a student was trying to divide 12 by 3, he or she could use the portion of a number line from 0 – 12 and work to split that section into three equal parts. Once split, the student would visually see that each part contains four numbers, making 4 the quotient of 12 and 3.

## USING DRAWINGS TO MODEL THE SUBTRACTION OF WHOLE NUMBERS

Students can use drawings to model the subtraction of whole numbers from a very young age. Suppose a student is trying to find the difference of 5 and 3. The student can draw five objects, and then cross out three of them. This allows the student to visually see that when three objects are taken away from five objects, two objects remain. In other words, the student has modeled that 5 – 3 = 2. This is the first step in teaching the concept of subtraction to young learners.

## USING CONCRETE MODELING EXAMPLE

A teacher allows her students to use unit cubes while completing addition and subtracting problems. Discuss the type of modeling that is taking place.

> The teacher is providing students with the opportunity to use concrete modeling to complete their addition and subtraction problems. Concrete modeling is often used with young students or students who are struggling to grasp the concepts of addition or subtraction. With concrete modeling, students act out the problems. For example, if a student is challenged with finding the sum of 5 and 8, the student can create a pile of 5 cubes, along with a pile of 8 cubes. The student can then count the total number of cubes in both piles to find the sum of 5 and 8. Similarly, if a student is struggling to find the difference of 9 and 3, the student can create a pile of 9 cubes. The student would then take 3 cubes away, and count the numbers of cubes that remain. This would allow the student to truly see what remains when 3 objects are taken away from 9 objects.

## RECTANGULAR ARRAYS AND AREA MODELS

Rectangular arrays and area models are both used to help students visualize the multiplication of two whole numbers. However, the models are used at different levels of multiplication proficiency. Traditionally, students begin to conceptualize the idea of multiplication using rectangular arrays. As students become more proficient, they progress to area models. Let's consider the multiplication of 4 and 5. A student still developing the concept of multiplication can create a rectangular array to find the product. To do so, the student can draw a row of 4 objects, such as stars, to represent the first set. Since the problem is 4 times 5, the student can then draw identical rows above or below their first row, until they have 5 rows of 4 identical stars. When complete, the student can count the total number of stars to find that 4 times 5 equals 20. A more advanced learner can adjust this strategy by drawing a rectangle and labeling the top with a 4 and the side with a 5. The student can then break the rectangle into four parts vertically, and 5 parts horizontally. After counting the boxes, the student has modeled that 4 times 5 equals 20.

## PARTITIONING METHOD EXAMPLE

Explain the process for using the partitioning method to multiply 34 times 25.

> The partitioning method is used to help students visualize the true value of larger numbers, and helps them to mentally calculate these numbers. The process for applying the partitioning method is to break apart each number and multiply each part separately. Then students must find the sum of each part to find the total product. For a problem such as 34 times 25, the student would multiply 30 by 20, which is 600, and 30 by 5, which is 150. Then the student would multiply 4 by 20, which is 80, and 4 by 5, which is 20. Finally, the student would find the sum of the partitioned products, 600 + 150 + 80 + 20, to find that the product of 34 and 25 is 850.

## AREA MODEL EXAMPLE

Describe the process for drawing an area model to represent the product of 24 and 18.

The area model is used to find the product of multi-digit numbers by writing each factor in expanded form. To create an area model for the product of 24 and 18, we must break 24 into 20 + 4, and 18 into 10 + 8. Then we draw a rectangle broken into four parts. Along the top, we write the number 20 above the first column and the number 4 above the second column. Along the side, we label the top row 10, and the bottom row 8. We fill in each empty box by multiplying the top and side numbers of each cell. For example, top left cell should contain the number 200 to show the product of 20 and 10. Following this logic, the top right cell should contain the product 40 (4 times 10), and the bottom row should contain the products 160 (20 times 8), and 32 (8 times 4). Our last step is to add all the products in the cells we have completed. The sum of 200 + 40 + 160 + 32 is 432, making the product of 24 and 18 equal to 432.

## DECOMPOSITION STRATEGY OR COMPENSATION STRATEGY EXAMPLE

Identify and describe two different strategies that can be used to multiply 39 by 12.

To multiply 39 and 12, we can use the decomposition strategy or the compensation strategy. Using the decomposition strategy we can rewrite 39 as 30 + 9. Then we multiply each part of the expanded form by 12 and add our products together. Since 30 times 12 is 360, and 9 times 12 is 108, we can add 360 and 108 to find our final product of 468. On the other hand, using the compensation strategy we can round 39 to the compatible number of 40. When we multiply 40 by 12, we get 480. Next, we must determine how much bigger our estimate is from our actual product. Since 40 is one more than 39, we must multiply 1 by 12, which is 12. That means our estimation is 12 more than our actual product. The difference of 480 and 12 is 468, again proving our final product to be 468.

## INTERPRETING THE REMAINDER EXAMPLE

Henry has $15.00. Determine the number of $2.00 candy bars that can Henry buy. Explain your process and discuss how you would help students to interpret the remainder in problems similar to this.

To determine the number of candy bars Henry can purchase we need to divide $15.00 by $2.00, or more simply, 15 by 2. The quotient of 15 and 2 is 7.5. This means that Henry can buy 7 candy bars. This type of problem assesses a student's understanding of remainders. Most students will realize that they cannot go into a store and buy half a candy bar. However, following the traditional rules of rounding, 7.5 would round up to 8, tricking some students into thinking the answer should be 8 candy bars. To help students interpret this problem correctly you can ask students to check their answers by multiplying the number of candy bars Henry plans on buying by $2.00, to be sure their total is less than $15.00, the amount of money Henry has. You can also have a discussion about the real-world. Ask students questions such as "Is it okay to have more money than you owe?" Or "Is it okay to have less money than you owe?" Presenting word problems as real-world situations helps students to interpret what to do with remainders in different types of situations.

## DETERMINING CHANGE EXAMPLES

Kyle purchases three movie tickets, each of which costs $9.00. Determine how much change Kyle will receive if he pays with two $20.00 bills. Explain your process.

13

To begin, we must determine how much money Kyle will be charged for the three movie tickets. If each movie ticket costs $9.00, then three movie tickets will cost Kyle $27.00 (since $9 \times 3 = 27$). Next, we must determine how much money Kyle has to spend. Kyle has two $20.00 bills. Since 20 times 2 equals 40, we know Kyle has a total of $40.00. Our final step is to subtract the cost of the tickets ($27.00) from the amount of money Kyle has to spend ($40.00). The difference of 40 and 27 is 13, meaning Kyle will receive $13.00 in change after purchasing three movie tickets.

Three friends are splitting the cost of a $12.00 pizza. Each friend has a $5.00 bill to contribute. Calculate how much change each friend should receive. Explain your process.

In this example we have a total bill of $12.00 being split three equal ways. The word "split" tells us to divide 12 by 3, which is 4. This means each friend owes $4.00 towards the bill. If each friend contributes a $5.00 bill, but only owes $4.00, we need to find the difference of $5.00 and $4.00 to determine the amount of change each friend will receive. The difference of 5 and 4 is 1, meaning each friend should receive $1.00 in change after paying his or her share of the bill.

## WORDS OR PHRASES INDICATING ADDITION IS NEEDED TO SOLVE WORD PROBLEMS

There are many words or phrases that are used to indicate addition is needed to solve a word problem. These words include but are not limited to: *sum, altogether, in all, in total, increase, plus, longer than, above,* or *more than.* In contrast, there are many words or phrases that indicate subtraction as the needed operation. These words include but are not limited to: *difference, fewer than, how many more, less, minus, remain, decrease, take away, shorter than, below,* or *remove.* It is important that students are fluent with identifying these words as operational indicators so that they can quickly and efficiently solve word problems. Teachers can provide recognition practice by providing opportunities for games such as word sorts, matching games, or flashcards.

## DETERMINING HEIGHT EXAMPLE

Andre is six inches taller than Collin. Determine Andre's height if Collin is 54 inches tall.

In this example we know that Andre is taller than Collin, so Andre's height will be greater than Collin's height. To start, we need to identify the important information the problem gives us. We know that Collin is 54 inches tall. We also know that Andre is six inches taller, or in other words, Andres's height is six inches *more than* Collin's height. The phrase "more than" indicates addition, so we need to add 6 inches to Collin's height of 54 inches in order to find Andre's height. Since $54 + 6 = 60$, we can determine that Andre is 60 inches tall.

## CONNECTION BETWEEN MULTIPLICATION AND REPEATED ADDITION

Multiplication can be thought of as a more sophisticated form of repeated addition. In fact, when learning the concept of multiplication, students are encouraged to think of multiplication as repeated addition. Let's use 3 times 5 as an example. When first exploring multiplication, students are presented with various ways to visualize 3 times 5 as five groups of threes. Teachers might provide students opportunities to create, manipulate, and explore concrete models, graphic representations, and eventually rectangular arrays to determine these products. As students gain fact fluency, it is the goal that repeated addition be relied on less, while memorized multiplication facts become a requirement. The transition from repeated addition to multiplication fact fluency is an important step in the development of skills, since multiplication is a much more efficient way of calculating values as math concepts become more complex.

## INVERSE OPERATIONS

The term "inverse operations" refers to the operations that are opposite each other. In other words, inverse operations are the operations that undo or "balance" each other. The inverse operation of addition is subtraction, while the inverse operation of subtraction is addition. On the other hand, the inverse operation of multiplication is division, while the inversion operation of division is multiplication. Inverse operations are often used when solving equations in an effort to isolate the variable and determine its value.

## FRACTIONS EXAMPLE

*Convert the fraction $\frac{1}{5}$ to a decimal. Explain your process.*

There are many ways to convert a fraction to a decimal. At times, a fraction may have a denominator that is a factor of some power-of-ten. In these instances, you can rewrite the fraction as an equivalent fraction with a denominator of 10, 100, 1000, etc. Here, 5 is a factor of 10, so we can rewrite $\frac{1}{5}$ as $\frac{2}{10}$. The fraction $\frac{2}{10}$ is read "two tenths," which can be written in decimal form as 0.2. When dealing with a fraction that does not easily convert to a power-of-ten denominator, we can convert a fraction to a decimal by dividing the numerator by the denominator. Using the rules of long division, we can conclude that $1 \div 5 = 0.2$, therefore $\frac{1}{5}$ is equivalent to 0.2.

*Convert the fraction $\frac{3}{20}$ to a percent. Explain your process.*

The term "percent" means "per 100." One strategy for converting a fraction to a percent is to rewrite the fraction as an equivalent fraction with a denominator of 100. Here, $\frac{3}{20}$ can be rewritten as $\frac{15}{100}$. Once you have a denominator of 100, the numerator can be written with the percent sign. Therefore, $\frac{3}{20}$, or $\frac{15}{100}$, is equivalent to 15%. If you have a denominator that is not a factor of 100 you can divide the numerator by the denominator, then multiply your answer by 100. Keeping with our example, we can divide 3 by 20, which gives us a quotient of 0.15. Then, we multiply by 100 (quick trick for multiplying a number by 100: move the decimal point two places to the right). The product of 0.15 and 100 is 15; therefore $\frac{3}{20}$ is the same as 15%.

Express the ratio 6:7 as a fraction. Explain your reasoning.

When expressing a ratio as a fraction, we write the first number of the ratio as the numerator over the second number of the ratio as the denominator. In other words, $a:b$ can be expressed as the ratio $\frac{a}{b}$. In our example, 6:7 can be expressed as $\frac{6}{7}$. We can reduce ratios the same way we would reduce fractions, with the exception of mixed numbers. If a ratio creates an improper fraction, that ratio must remain an improper fraction (never a mixed number) in order to accurately represent the relationship that exists between the two values.

*Discuss how the fraction $\frac{22}{8}$ can be used to determine how many slices of a pizza pie each member of a 22-person team will receive.*

A fraction bar is technically a division sign. Therefore, this fraction is representing the expression **22 ÷ 8**. We already know that the number 22 represents the number of people, so 8 must represent the number of whole pizzas that are being shared. We can use our knowledge of reducing fractions to avoid long division. We can rewrite $\frac{22}{8}$ as a mixed number by determining that 8 fits into 22 twice, with 6 left over. In more mathematical terms, $\frac{22}{8}$ reduces to $2\frac{6}{8}$, or $2\frac{3}{4}$. Therefore, each person will receive $2\frac{3}{4}$ slices of pizza.

*Josephine determined that she had enough wire to make $3\frac{3}{4}$ bracelets. Discuss how the fraction $\frac{3}{4}$ should be interpreted in this situation.*

In a situation such as this, we need to think about what our remainder truly represents. Here, it represents extra wire to make part of a bracelet. Since wire that is too short to form a whole bracelet will most likely create a bracelet that doesn't fit, it is illogical to begin a fourth bracelet at all. Therefore, although Josephine has enough wire to make $3\frac{3}{4}$ bracelets, the remaining $\frac{3}{4}$ wire is not enough for a fourth bracelet and should be discarded or saved for some other project. When answering a question such as this, we should be careful to interpret the remainder appropriately and state that Josephine has enough wire to make three bracelets.

*Describe the process for drawing an area model to show the product of $\frac{1}{3} \times \frac{2}{5}$.*

When we multiply a fraction by a fraction, we are finding a part of a part, meaning our product will always be less than either of our factors. Using modeling can help students to understand this concept. To model the multiplication of $\frac{1}{3} \times \frac{2}{5}$ we start by drawing a rectangle. Since our first fraction is $\frac{1}{3}$, we need to draw horizontal lines breaking the rectangle into three equal parts, with one of the parts shaded. The second factor of our problem is $\frac{2}{5}$. Now it's time to break our rectangle into five equal parts vertically, with two of those five parts shaded. The product of $\frac{1}{3} \times \frac{2}{5}$ is shown in the portion of the rectangle that has been shaded both vertically and horizontally. Here, our rectangle now has 15 total parts, with only three of them shaded both vertically and horizontally. This models the product of $\frac{1}{3} \times \frac{2}{5}$ as $\frac{2}{15}$.

## USING A NUMBER LINE TO MODEL THE MULTIPLICATION OF A FRACTION AND A WHOLE NUMBER

A number line can be used to help students visualize the multiplication of fractions and whole numbers using carefully created number lines and skip counting. For example, the product of $\frac{1}{4}$ and 5 really means $\frac{1}{4}$, five times. To visualize this on a number line, students can create a number line broken into fourths ($\frac{1}{4}, \frac{2}{4}, \frac{3}{4}, \frac{4}{4}$ or 1 whole, $\frac{5}{4}$ or $1\frac{1}{4}$, etc.). Once the number line is created, students can start at zero and draw arrows to show five "jumps" along each $\frac{1}{4}$ hash mark. After students have taken 5 jumps, they should arrive at $1\frac{1}{4}$. Using the number line, students can see why $\frac{1}{4} \times 5 = 1\frac{1}{4}$.

## UNIT FRACTIONS

A unit fraction is a fraction with a numerator of 1 and a denominator of any whole number. Some examples of unit fractions include $\frac{1}{2}, \frac{1}{3}, \frac{1}{4}, \frac{1}{5}$, and so on. Unit fractions are important for many reasons. A student's first experience with fractions usually involves unit fractions in an effort to help visualize what a part of a whole really looks like. As students develop their understanding of fractions, unit fractions are often used to show how different fractions compare to one another. For example, $\frac{1}{3}$ of a pizza is much greater than $\frac{1}{8}$ of that same pizza. It is here that students discover the new concept of larger numbers representing smaller amounts. Unit fractions help students to visualize that fractions with equivalent numerators follow an unusual rule: the larger the denominator, the smaller the piece. Furthermore, unit fractions lead students to understand other fractions. For example, students can visualize $\frac{3}{4}$ as three one-fourths. A strong grasp of unit fractions can help a learner to develop other skills such as division and multiplication of fractions more quickly than a learner who struggles with these fundamental basics.

## PROCESS FOR DECOMPOSING FRACTIONS

When we decompose a fraction, we are simply breaking that fraction into smaller pieces. Most commonly, we decompose a fraction to represent a sum of its unit fractions. For example, to decompose $\frac{5}{8}$ we can use the unit fraction $\frac{1}{8}$. Since $\frac{5}{8}$ consists of five one-eighths, we can decompose $\frac{5}{8}$ as $\frac{1}{8} + \frac{1}{8} + \frac{1}{8} + \frac{1}{8} + \frac{1}{8}$. Decomposing fractions helps students to visualize the value of different fractions, especially when dealing with improper fractions. For example, being able to visualize $\frac{5}{3}$ as $\frac{1}{3} + \frac{1}{3} + \frac{1}{3} + \frac{1}{3} + \frac{1}{3}$ is helpful in seeing how much bigger $\frac{5}{3}$ is than one whole. It is also helpful in developing the concept of how much a fraction truly represents. For example, a student who can visualize $\frac{6}{7}$ as six one-sevenths is more likely to abstractly determine that $\frac{6}{7}$ is greater than $\frac{1}{2}$.

## DECOMPOSING FRACTIONS EXAMPLE

*Tara states that she can decompose the fraction $\frac{4}{5}$ as $\frac{1}{5} + \frac{1}{5} + \frac{1}{5}$. Identify and correct her error.*

When we decompose a fraction, we break that fraction into a sum of its parts. Here, Tara was correct in breaking her fraction down into the unit fraction $\frac{1}{5}$. Her error lies in the number of fifths she has included in her number sentence. Tara's decomposition of $\frac{4}{5}$ is written $\frac{1}{5} + \frac{1}{5} + \frac{1}{5}$. This expression only has a value of $\frac{3}{5}$. To correct her mistake, Tara must add an additional $\frac{1}{5}$ to her number sentence. The true decomposition of $\frac{4}{5}$ should be written $\frac{1}{5}+\frac{1}{5}+\frac{1}{5}+\frac{1}{5}$.

## RULE TO FOLLOW FOR ORDERING UNIT FRACTIONS

A unit fraction is a fraction that has a numerator of 1 and a denominator of any whole number, such as $\frac{1}{2}, \frac{1}{3}$ or $\frac{1}{4}$. When visualizing unit fractions it helps to envision your favorite pie. If you were sharing your pie with only one other person, you could eat $\frac{1}{2}$ of that pie. However, if you were to share that pie with a total of ten people, you'd only indulge in $\frac{1}{10}$ of that same pie. The fewer people you share the whole pie with, the larger the piece you will receive. This leads us to our rule for ordering unit fractions. When dealing with unit fractions, the smaller denominators represent the greater values, while the greater denominators represent the smaller values. Therefore, unit fractions from least to greatest would be listed as $\frac{1}{5}, \frac{1}{4}, \frac{1}{3}, \frac{1}{2}$.

## ORDERING UNIT FRACTIONS EXAMPLES

*Order the following unit fractions from least to greatest: $\frac{1}{5}, \frac{1}{7}, \frac{1}{3}, \frac{1}{8}, \frac{1}{2}$. Discuss your reasoning.*

From least to greatest the fractions should be ordered $\frac{1}{8}, \frac{1}{7}, \frac{1}{5}, \frac{1}{3}, \frac{1}{2}$. When dealing with unit fractions we must remember that the larger the denominator is, the smaller the value it represents. Therefore, if you are ordering unit fractions from least to greatest, you can simply order your denominators from greatest to least. This will ensure that your smallest values are at the front of your list, with your greatest values at the end of your list. If you are ever unsure of whether a unit fraction is greater than another unit fraction simply compare their denominators. The fraction with the larger denominator has the smaller value.

## DETERMINING WHICH FRACTION IS LARGER EXAMPLE

*Consider the fractions $\frac{2}{7}$ and $\frac{1}{5}$. Explain how equivalent fractions can be used to determine which fraction is larger. Determine which fraction is larger.*

Equivalent fractions are used to compare fractions because they create a situation in which both fractions represent the same whole. To compare $\frac{2}{7}$ and $\frac{1}{5}$ using equivalent fractions, we must determine the least common denominator, or LCD. The LCD is the least common multiple of the denominators. The LCD of 7 and 5 is 35. Next, we must determine our new numerators. Let's start by writing $\frac{2}{7}=\frac{x}{35}$. To determine $x$, we must determine the factor by which the denominator, 7, is multiplied by to arrive at the LCD. For 7 to increase to 35, it must be multiplied by 5, so we know our new fraction is five times bigger than $\frac{2}{7}$. To keep our values equivalent, we multiply our numerator by the same factor as our denominator. The product of 2 and 5 is 10, so our new numerator must be 10. That makes our equivalent fraction $\frac{10}{35}$. Using similar logic we can conclude that $\frac{1}{5}=\frac{7}{35}$. Now that we have equivalent fractions with common denominators, $\frac{10}{35}$ and $\frac{7}{35}$, we can compare the numerators. Since 10 is greater than 7, we can conclude that $\frac{10}{35}$ is greater than $\frac{7}{35}$, or that $\frac{2}{7}$ is greater than $\frac{1}{5}$.

## CREATING EQUIVALENT FRACTIONS EXAMPLE

*Create equivalent fractions to write an inequality comparing $\frac{3}{5}$ and $\frac{5}{9}$. Explain your process.*

In order to create equivalent fractions for $\frac{3}{5}$ and $\frac{5}{9}$ we must first determine our least common denominator, or LCD. Here, the LCD of 5 and 9 is 45. Let's start by writing $\frac{3}{5}$ = $\frac{x}{45}$. The original denominator, 5, must have been multiplied by a factor of 9 to arrive at 45, so in order to keep our fractions equivalent, we must multiply our numerator, 3, by 9 as well. That makes our new fraction $\frac{27}{45}$. We can repeat the process to determine that $\frac{5}{9} = \frac{25}{45}$. Now that we have equivalent fractions, $\frac{27}{45}$ and $\frac{25}{45}$, we can compare their values. Our denominators are equivalent, which means that to compare their values, we can simply compare their numerators. Since 27 is greater than 25, we can conclude that $\frac{27}{45}$ is greater than $\frac{25}{45}$. Using our original fractions and an inequality symbol we can also represent this as $\frac{3}{5} > \frac{5}{9}$.

## USING THE SAME WHOLE WHEN COMPARING FRACTIONS

When comparing fractions, it is important that each fraction is part of the same whole. Otherwise, the comparisons, both visually and mathematically, can be perceived inaccurately. Let's say we are comparing the fractions $\frac{1}{2}$ and $\frac{1}{8}$ using visual models. We have chosen to use a dime to represent $\frac{1}{2}$ and a large pizza to represent $\frac{1}{8}$. In this example, $\frac{1}{2}$ of a dime is a considerably smaller area than $\frac{1}{8}$ of a pizza pie. That might confuse us into thinking that $\frac{1}{2}$ is less than $\frac{1}{8}$, which is not true. In order to compare these fractions accurately, we must use the same whole for each representation. Now, let's use a pizza to compare *both* fractions. Visualize two pizzas, both of equal size. In one pizza, $\frac{1}{2}$ of the pizza is shaded. In the other pizza, $\frac{1}{8}$ of the pizza is shaded. When visualizing the same whole, it is easy to conclude that $\frac{1}{2}$ is greater than $\frac{1}{8}$.

## COMPARING FRACTIONS EXAMPLE

*A child draws two rectangles. He shades $\frac{1}{4}$ of the first rectangle and $\frac{1}{2}$ of the second rectangle. Based on his picture, he concludes that $\frac{1}{4}$ is greater than $\frac{1}{2}$. Identify and correct his error.*

The student did not represent fractions from the same whole. If his drawing shows $\frac{1}{4}$ to be greater than $\frac{1}{2}$, than the whole rectangle used to represent $\frac{1}{4}$ must have been considerably larger than the whole rectangle used to represent $\frac{1}{2}$. To correct his error, the student must draw two rectangles of equal size. Then he can shade $\frac{1}{4}$ of one rectangle and $\frac{1}{2}$ of the other. This will ensure that he is comparing fractions of the same whole, allowing him to visualize and conclude that $\frac{1}{4}$ is, in fact, less than $\frac{1}{2}$.

## FRACTIONS WITH IDENTICAL NUMERATOR AND DENOMINATOR

Any fraction with an identical numerator and denominator is equivalent to one whole, or simply 1. When envisioning fractions, the denominator tells us how many pieces the whole is broken into. The numerator tells us how many of those parts are shaded or represented. Let's pretend we are selling a pie at a bake sale. Our pie is cut into six slices and we sell six slices of our pie. If each slice represents $\frac{1}{6}$ of the pie, and we have sold six slices, then we have sold $\frac{6}{6}$ of our entire pie. In other words, we have sold one whole pie, which can be represented as 1. That makes $\frac{6}{6}$ = 1. We can conclude that any fraction containing equivalent numerators and denominators can be expressed as one whole, or 1.

## IDENTICAL NUMERATOR AND DENOMINATOR EXAMPLE

*Together, Dan and Dayna ate $\frac{8}{8}$ of a pizza. Represent this amount without using a fraction. Explain your reasoning.*

> Anytime a fraction contains a numerator that is equivalent to its denominator, that fraction can be reduced to one whole, which we can express as 1. Here, Dan and Dayna ordered a pizza. We know that the pizza was cut into 8 slices because the denominator is 8. Our numerator tells us that Dan and Dayna consumed 8 slices. If 8 of the 8 slices have been eaten, then we know that the entire pizza has been eaten. Rather than saying Dan and Dayna ate $\frac{8}{8}$ of a pizza, we can simply say that Dan and Dayna ate one whole pizza, which we can represent as the whole number 1.

## WRITING WHOLE NUMBERS AS FRACTIONS

To write a whole number as a fraction we can simply write our whole number as our numerator over a denominator of 1. For example, if we want to express the number 3 as a fraction, we can write $\frac{3}{1}$. Conceptually, our denominator, 1, tells us that our whole is split into only one piece. Our numerator tells us that three of those one pieces are shaded or represented. If each whole only allows us to shade one part, then we need three wholes to shade three parts. That makes $\frac{3}{1}$ = 3 wholes, or simply 3.

## WRITING WHOLE NUMBERS AS FRACTIONS EXAMPLE

*Explain why $\frac{6}{1}$ is equivalent to 6.*

> The denominator of any fraction tells us how many pieces our "whole" is divided into. Here, our denominator is 1, meaning our whole is simply one whole. Each whole is not divided into smaller pieces. The numerator of any fraction tells us how many parts of our whole should be shaded or represented. Here, our numerator is six. Any time our numerator is greater than our denominator, we have an improper fraction, meaning we have more than one whole. If we were to draw rectangles to model $\frac{6}{1}$, and each rectangle could only represent one of the six shaded pieces, which means we would need six whole rectangles to represent $\frac{6}{1}$. This is why $\frac{6}{1}$ can also be expressed as the whole number 6.

# Algebraic Thinking

## EXTENDING A PATTERN EXAMPLES

Consider the number set 3, 9, 27, 81. Describe the pattern and find the next term of the sequence.

> Before we can extend any pattern, we need to analyze the sequence that is presented to us and determine how the terms are related to one another. Here, we

notice that each term is three times more than the previous term. In other words, each term is multiplied by three in order to find the next term in the sequence. The last term is 81, so we need to multiply 81 by 3 in order to extend the pattern. Since 81 × 3 = 243, the next term in the pattern must be 243.

Describe the pattern and find the next three shapes of the following sequence: triangle, rectangle, pentagon, hexagon.

After analyzing the attributes of each shape in the pattern, we notice that the pattern is based on the number of sides that each term is comprised of. A triangle has three sides, a rectangle has four sides, a pentagon has five sides, and a hexagon has six sides. Keeping with this logic, we know the next three terms must be polygons made up of 7, 8, and 9 sides. A seven-sided polygon is a heptagon. An eight-sided polygon is an octagon, and a nine-sided polygon is a nonagon. That makes the next three terms in our sequence a heptagon, an octagon, and a nonagon.

## CONJECTURE

In mathematics, a conjecture is a guess or speculation that we make based on incomplete information. With conjectures, we speculate to make sense of things, based on patterns we may notice or anticipate. A student may be asked to make a conjecture about the pattern 5, 10, 16, 23, 31. In response, the student might make the conjecture that each term increases by 5, 6, 7, 8, etc. When studying more advanced mathematics, people make conjectures that apply to the number system as a whole, most commonly in the areas of geometry and algebra. Arguably the most common conjecture is the Pythagorean Theorem, which is used to find the side length of a triangle, when two other side lengths are known. The theorem states that $a^2 + b^2 = c^2$, where $c$ represents the length of the hypotenuse, and $a$ and $b$ represent the side lengths of the other two legs of the triangle.

> **Review Video: Similar Triangles**
> Visit mometrix.com/academy and enter code: 398538

## CONJECTURE EXAMPLE

Julia realizes that her teacher has given pop quizzes after chapters 3, 6, and 9 of their current novel. Hypothesize when Julia can expect another pop quiz. Explain your reasoning.

Julia's teacher has given a pop quiz after chapters 3, 6, and 9. It seems as though each quiz occurs after a multiple of 3, or in other words, each quiz occurs three chapters after the previous quiz. In order to hypothesize when the next pop quiz will be, Julia can find the next multiple of 3, or simply add 3 to the last term of the sequence. Since 9 + 3 is 12, it is reasonable to assume that Julia can expect her next pop quiz after chapter 12.

## DIAGONAL PATTERNS FOUND IN THE ADDITION TABLE

From the top left corner to the bottom right corner of any addition table, we can see that the diagonal contains the multiples of 2 (2, 4, 6, 8, etc.). The reason for this is because as we move one digit to the right and one digit down, we are always increasing our sum by 2. Considering any diagonal from the top right to bottom left corner of the addition table, we can see that our diagonals include identical numbers. This is because as we move left in the table, we are subtracting one from our value; however, as we move down in the table, we add one to our value. The process of both subtracting and adding one to any value will always result in the original number.

21

## PATTERNS AND TERMS EXAMPLES

Explain the pattern and find the next three terms for the following number sequence: 1, 5, 4, 8, 7, 11, 10...

> In this pattern, the rule alternates between adding four and subtracting one. In other words, the pattern for the first six terms of this sequence is +4, −1, +4, −1, +4, −1. To continue the pattern, we must add 4 to our last term, 10. That makes the 7th term in the pattern 14. Next, we must subtract 1, which leads us to the eighth term of our pattern, 13, because 14 − 1 = 13. Finally, we must again add 4 to our last term in order to find our ninth term. Since 13 + 4 = 17, we know the ninth term must be 17. That makes the next three terms of the sequence 14, 13, 17.

Explain the pattern and find the next three terms for the following number sequence: 3, 9, 7, 21, 19, 57...

> Here we have another example of a pattern in which the rule alternates. In this sequence, our terms are tripled, then decreased by two. In other words, the first six terms of this sequence follow the pattern × 3, −2, × 3, −2, × 3, −2. To find the seventh term, we must continue the alternating pattern and decrease 57 by 2. That makes our seventh term 55. Next, we must triple 55 to find our eighth term. The product of 55 and 3 is 165, so our eighth term is 165. Finally, we can find our ninth term by subtracting 2 from 165, which results in 163. The next three terms of the pattern are 55, 165, 163.

## MENTALLY MULTIPLYING EXAMPLES

*Discuss how the commutative property can be applied to mentally multiply* $5 \times 14 \times 4$.

> When multiplying large numbers mentally, it helps to look for compatible numbers. Compatible numbers are numbers that are easy to calculate mentally, and result in answers that are easy to work with. We can find the product of $5 \times 14 \times 4$ by applying the commutative property in order to move compatible numbers closer together. In this expression, we can use our principles of commutativity to rewrite the expression as $5 \times 4 \times 14$. That allows us to mentally multiply 5 and 4 first, resulting in a product of 20. Then, we can use our mental math skills to multiply 14 and 20, which is 280. By using the commutative property and our knowledge of compatible numbers, we can mentally calculate that $5 \times 14 \times 4$ equals 280.

Determine how the distributive property can be used to mentally multiply 57 and 6.

> We can use the distributive property to multiply larger numbers by breaking them apart and then bringing them back together. To multiply 57 and 6 using the distributive property, we first need to think of 57 in expanded form, as 50 + 7. Then we can multiply each part of 57 by 6. We can start by multiplying 50 and 6, which is 300. Then, we can multiply 7 by 6, which is 42. Finally, we must add our products, 300 and 42, together to find our final product of 342. Using the distributive property we are able to mentally calculate that $57 \times 6 = 342$.

---

**Review Video: Commutative, Associative, and Distributive Property**
Visit mometrix.com/academy and enter code: 483176

---

## MENTALLY ADDING EXAMPLES

Explain how the associative property can be used to mentally add (78 + 16) + 4.

Using the associative property can prove helpful when trying to mentally calculate numerical expressions. Here, we have the expression (78 + 16) + 4. Adding 78 and 16 could be challenging, but if we look at our other addends we notice that 16 and 4 are compatible numbers. This means they are easily calculated and result in a sum, 20, that is easy to work with. By applying the associative property, we can think of this expression as 78 + (16 + 4). After finding the sum of 16 and 4, which is 20, we can add the final addend, 78. Since 78 + 20 = 98, we can mentally calculate that (78 + 16) + 4 equals 98.

## PURPOSE AND SEQUENCE FOR THE ORDER OF OPERATIONS

The order of operations provides the sequence we must follow when simplifying different parts of an expression. If an expression is solved and the order of operations is not followed, the expression will not be simplified correctly, resulting in an incorrect answer. When simplifying an expression using the order of operations, many people using the acronym PEMDAS, where each letter stands for a different step to follow. Parentheses are always the first part of an expression to be solved. When there is more than one operation inside the parentheses, the order of operations should be followed within the parentheses as well. Next, all exponents should be simplified. Once that is taken care of, all multiplication and division must be solved, from left to right in the order in which they appear. Finally, all addition and subtraction should be simplified, again from left to right. If these operations are simplified in the correct sequence, the value of the expression will be accurate.

> **Review Video: Adding and Subtracting with Exponents**
> Visit mometrix.com/academy and enter code: 875756

## ORDER OF OPERATIONS EXAMPLES

In multistep number sentences, Georgie always solves multiplication before division. Explain Georgie's error and explain the rule for solving multiplication and division in the same number sentence.

Georgie is making a common mistake. Using the acronym PEMDAS, many students believe that multiplication should always come before division, because the M is before the D in the acronym. This is not the case. When solving an expression using the order of operations, inverse operations are solved in the order in which they appear, from left to right. First, all multiplication and division must be simplified. Then, all addition and subtraction can be simplified. A strategy for helping Georgie might be to have him write the acronym "PEMDAS" at the top of his page, with two circles. He can draw one circle around the M and the D, and another circle around the A and the S. This would serve as a visual reminder for Georgie to look for multiplication and division at the same time (from left to right), followed by addition and subtraction at the same time.

> **Review Video: Order of Operations**
> Visit mometrix.com/academy and enter code: 259675

*Using the order of operations, find the value of $2^3 \div 4 + 5 - 2 \times 3$. Explain your process.*

This expression does not contain any parentheses, so we can start by simplifying the exponent, $2^3$. The base number is 2, with an exponent of 3, meaning we need to calculate $2 \times 2 \times 2$, which equals 8. This simplifies our expression to $8 \div 4 + 5 - 2$ x 3. Next, we must simplify all multiplication and division, from left to right. Here, division comes before multiplication in the expression, so we must first simplify $8 \div 4$, which is 2. Our expression is now simplified to $2 + 5 - 2$ x 3. We're now ready to simplify the multiplication, 2 x 3, which is 6. At this point, our simplified expression is $2 + 5 - 6$. Again, our inverse operations are simplified from left to right. Here, addition is presented before subtraction, so we can add $2 + 5$, which is 7. Our final expression is $7 - 6$, which equals 1. Following the order of operations, we can simplify the expression $2^3 \div 4 + 5 - 2$ x 3 to 1.

*Evaluate $50 - (4 \times 5 - 2) \div 3 + 3^2$. Explain your process.*

When following the order of operations, we must start with our parentheses. Here, our parentheses contain both multiplication and subtraction. When we have more than one operation in the parentheses, we must follow the order of operations *within* the parentheses. Since multiplication is simplified before subtraction in the order of operations, we'll start there. The product of 4 and 5 is 20, and two less than 20 is 18. Therefore, our parentheses simplify to 18. That makes our new expression $50 - 18 \div 3 + 3^2$. Next, we must simplify our exponent, $3^2$, which is equivalent to 9. Our new expression is now $50 - 18 \div 3 + 9$. The next step in the order of operations is to look for multiplication and division. In this expression, we only have division, so we can simplify $18 \div 3$, which is 6. We now have the expression $50 - 6 + 9$. Finally, we must simplify all addition and subtraction from left to right. Since subtraction is presented before addition, we must first find the difference of 50 and 6, which is 44. Finally, we have simplified our expression to $44 + 9$, or 53. Using the order of operations we know that $50 - (4 \times 5 - 2) \div 3 + 3^2$ equals 53.

## WRITING AND SOLVING EQUATIONS EXAMPLES

Together, Sienna and Liv beaded a total of 42 bracelets. If Sienna beaded 26 of them, write and solve an equation to find the number of bracelets Liv beaded.

When writing equations, we must look for key words that imply operations. The word "together" tells us that Sienna's and Liv's bracelets are being combined, which implies addition. We can start by writing our equations as words, such as "Sienna's bracelets + Liv's bracelets = the total number of bracelets." Next, we must replace our words with any numeric values that we are given. We know that Sienna beaded 26 of the bracelets; we also know that the total number of bracelets is 42. This allows us to rewrite our equation as 26 + Liv's bracelets = 42. We can use a variable to replace the unknown value to simplify our equation to $26 + x = 42$. To solve our equation, we must isolate the variable using inverse operations. The inverse operation of addition is subtraction, so we must subtract 26 from both sides of the equation. When we subtract 26 from the left side of the equation, we have isolated our variable, $x$. When we subtract 26 from the right side of our equation, we have a difference of 16. This means that $x = 16$. In other words, Liv beaded 16 of the bracelets.

At a bake sale, the cheerleading team sold $63.00 worth of pretzels. If each pretzel costs $3.00, write and solve an equation to find the number of pretzels sold.

Let's start by looking for key words that help us to identify the operation we need to include in our equation. Here, we know that each pretzel cost $3.00. When finding the total cost of several items, we need to multiply the cost by the quantity, so we'll need multiplication to write our equation. Next, we can think of our equation as the words "the price of each pretzel × the number of pretzels sold = the total amount of money collected." When we replace our words with numeric values from the problem, we have $3.00 × the number of pretzels sold = $63.00. Finally, we can write this algebraically, replacing the unknown value with a variable, such as $3.00$x$ = $63.00. To isolate our variable and find its value we must use the inverse operation of multiplication, which is division. When we divide the left side of our equation by $3.00, we're left with 1$x$, or more simply, $x$. When we divide the right side of our equation by $3.00, we find a quotient of 21. This tells us that $x = 21$. So the team sold 21 pretzels.

After the first round of a math competition, 28 students remained. If 4 students were eliminated in the first round, write and solve an equation to find the number of students that competed at the start of the tournament.

The key operational word found in this scenario is "eliminated," which implies subtraction. When can write this situation as "the number of students who started in the tournament – the number of students who were eliminated from the tournament = the number of students who remain in the tournament." Next, we can replace the parts of our equation with numeric values that we are given. We know that 28 students remain in the competition. We also know that 4 students were eliminated. This simplifies our equation to "the number of students who started in the tournament – 4 = 28." Let's replace our unknown value with a variable, writing our equation as $x – 4 = 28$. To solve, we must use the inverse operation of subtraction, which is addition. When we add 4 to both sides of our equation we are left with $x = 32$. This tells us that 32 students competed in the first round of the competition.

Mr. Hill wants to split his class into equal groups. Mr. Hill decides to create 7 groups, with each group containing 4 students. Write and solve an equation to find the number of students in Mr. Hill's class.

Here we have the key operational word "split," which tells us that we need to write an equation involving division. When we write our scenario as words used to describe the situation, we have, "The total number of students ÷ the number of students per group = the number of groups". Next, we can replace our words with numeric values, where possible. We know that Mr. Hill has 7 groups. We also know that each group has 4 students. We can now write our equation as "the total number of students ÷ 4 = 7", or $x ÷ 4 = 7$. When simplifying equations, we must isolate the variable using inverse operations. The inverse operation of division is multiplication, so we can multiply both sides of the equation by 4, leaving us with $x = 28$. There are 28 students in Mr. Hill's class.

Maggie's weekly allowance is $4.00 more than twice Austin's weekly allowance. If Maggie's weekly allowance is $20.00, write and solve an equation to find Austin's weekly allowance.

This scenario contains two sets of operational words or phrases. First, we have "more than," which implies addition. We also have "twice," which implies

25

multiplication by a factor of 2. We can make sense of this situation by writing our equation as "$4.00 + 2 × Austin's allowance = Maggie's allowance." We know that Maggie's allowance is $20.00, which simplifies our equation to $4.00 + 2 × Austin's allowance = $20.00, or more algebraically, $2x+\$4.00 = \$20.00$. Here, we have created a two-step equation. When isolating a variable with a two-step equation we must follow the order of operations *in reverse*, since we are trying to *undo* everything that has happened to the variable. This means we start by applying the inverse operation of addition, which is subtraction. When we subtract $4.00 from each side of the equation, we're left with $2x = \$16.00$. Finally, we're ready to isolate the variable by dividing both sides of the equation by 2. We know that that $x = \$8.00$. Austin's allowance is $8.00.

# Geometry, Measurement, and Data

## CLASSIFYING TRIANGLES BY THEIR ANGLES

Triangles can be classified based on the length of their sides, or the measure of their angles. It is important to know that every triangle contains three angles. The sum of these angles is always equivalent to 180 degrees. When classifying triangles by their angles, we must determine the measure of each angle. Once these measurements are known, we can describe any triangle as acute, obtuse, or right. If every angle in the triangle measures less than ninety degrees, the triangle is described as an acute triangle. If the triangle contains one obtuse angle (greater than 90 degrees), it is classified as an obtuse triangle. Finally, if the triangle contains one right angle (exactly 90 degrees), it is known as a right triangle.

## CLASSIFYING TRIANGLES BY THEIR SIDE LENGTHS

Every triangle is comprised of three straight lines, known as the triangle's sides. We can classify triangles based on the lengths of these sides. There are three options for classifying triangles by their side lengths. If a triangle has three side lengths of equal measure, the triangle is classified as an equilateral triangle. If the triangle has two side lengths of equal measure, it is known as an isosceles triangle. Finally, any triangle with no side lengths of equal measure is known as a scalene triangle.

## TRIANGLE AND SQUARE ATTRIBUTES

Triangles and squares are both polygons, meaning they are both enclosed shapes made up of straight lines, without any of those lines intersecting one another. Also, triangles and squares are both two-dimensional. However, a triangle is measured by its base and height, while a square is measured by its length and width. Triangles and squares also differ in the number of sides and angles they are comprised of. A triangle includes three sides and three angles, while a square includes four sides and four angles. A triangle can have angles and side lengths of any measure, while a square must have four right angles and four sides of equal length.

## LIST AND DESCRIBE THE NUMBER OF SHAPES THAT MUST BE INCLUDED ON THE NET OF A SQUARE PYRAMID.

A net is a two-dimensional drawing that is used to represent a three-dimensional shape. When drawing the net of a square pyramid, we can start by drawing the base. We can deduce that a square pyramid has a square base. This means we'll need to include a square in the net of our pyramid. From there, we can draw the sides of the pyramid. All pyramids have triangular sides. Since our base is a square, and a square has four sides, we will need to include four triangular sides in our net. In conclusion, the net of a square pyramid should include one square and four triangles.

## DECOMPOSING HEXAGONS USING TWO-DIMENSIONAL POLYGONS

Hexagons can be decomposed using two-dimensional figures in several ways. Younger learners can discover these decompositions using small manipulatives to "fill" a picture of a hexagon. One option for deconstruction a hexagon is to draw a line splitting the hexagon in half, creating two trapezoids. We can take this further by leaving one half a trapezoid, while breaking the other trapezoid into three small triangles. We also have the option of breaking both trapezoids into three triangles each, thus decomposing the hexagon into six small triangles. We can take this one step further by replacing two pairs of triangles with two rhombi. This would leave us with a hexagon decomposed using two rhombi and two triangles. Or, we could replace all six triangles with rhombi, constructing our hexagon of only three rhombi. Another option is to use one hexagon, one triangle, and one rhombus to deconstruct our hexagon.

> **Review Video: Polygons**
> Visit mometrix.com/academy and enter code: 271869

## THREE-DIMENSIONAL SHAPE EXAMPLE

A net contains only four triangles. Identify and explain which three-dimensional shape the net must represent.

> The net represents a triangular pyramid. We know this for several reasons. To start, a net containing all triangles must represent a pyramid, since all pyramids are three-dimensional figures comprised of only triangular sides. At least one shape of every net must represent the base. Here, we can conclude that the base is a triangle, since the net contains only triangles. If we know the shape has a triangular base, then we can infer the other three triangles represent three triangular sides. Any three-dimensional figure made up of a triangular base with three triangular sides must be a triangular pyramid.

## PARTITIONING POLYGONS

To partition a polygon means to break that polygon into smaller shapes, each of which can be arranged in way to fill the polygon exactly, without any overlapping parts. Younger learners can practice partitioning polygons using smaller manipulatives to fill the area of a larger area. For example, students can explore how four smaller triangles can be arranged to form one large triangle. Or, how four small squares can be used to form one large square. As students develop their mathematic abilities, partitioning is used as a strategy in advanced geometry to explore non-convex shapes as the sum of convex shapes for which they are comprised.

## EQUILATERAL TRIANGLE EXAMPLE

A hexagon is split into all equilateral triangles. Four of the triangles are shaded. In simplest form, determine what fraction of the hexagon is shaded.

> Any hexagon split into all equilateral triangles must contain six triangles. We know this because any other amount of equilateral triangles would result in a shape that is not classified as a hexagon. If four of those triangles are shaded, we can represent the shaded portion of the hexagon as $\frac{4}{6}$. In order to express this fraction in simplest form, we must divide the numerator and denominator by their greatest common factor, 2. When we divide both 4 and 6 by 2, we're left with the fraction $\frac{2}{3}$. The shaded portion of the hexagon can be represented using the fraction $\frac{2}{3}$.

## RECTANGLE EXAMPLES

A rectangle is split into six equal parts. Two of the parts are shaded. Explain, in simplest form, what fraction of the original rectangle is shaded.

> Regardless of the shape, any time we have an area split into equal parts, we can represent that shape using a fraction. Here, we have a rectangle split into six equal parts. This tells us our denominator must be six, since our denominator always represents the total number of parts in our whole. If two of those parts are shaded, we'll use the number 2 for our numerator. That leaves us with the fraction $\frac{2}{6}$. Since both 2 and 6 are divisible by 2, we can reduce this fraction to $\frac{1}{3}$. The shaded portion of our rectangle can be represented using the fraction $\frac{1}{3}$.

The volume of a rectangular prism is 60 cubic inches. The height of the prism is 5 inches and the length is 3 inches. Explain the process for writing an equation to find the missing dimension. Then, find the width of the prism using your equation.

> To start, we need to write the formula for finding the volume of a rectangular prism. The formula is volume = length × width × height. Next, we need to replace all components of the formula with the numeric values given to us. We are given the volume, height, and length of the prism, so we can rewrite our equation as 60 = 3 × width × 5. Using the commutative property, we can rearrange our expression to reflect 60 = 3 × 5 × width, allowing us to simplify our expression algebraically as 60 = 15$w$. To find the width of the prism, we must isolate our variable. To do so, we can divide both sides of our equation by 15. That leaves us with $w$ = 4. The width of the prism is 4 inches.

## MONEY PROBLEM EXAMPLE

While shopping at the mall, Dave purchased a hat for $19.48, socks for $7.36, and a shirt for $26.47. Calculate how much money Dave has remaining if he arrived at the mall with $75.00.

> To start, we must calculate the amount of money Dave spent at the mall. To do so, we must find the sum of $19.48, $7.36, and $26.47. When adding or subtracting decimals, it is important that we line up the decimal points, or stack them directly on top of one another. Then, we can add or subtract normally, bringing our decimal point straight down into our sum or difference. Here, when we add $19.48, $7.36, and $26.47, we find a sum of $53.31. Next, we must calculate the amount of money Dave has left after paying for his items. To subtract $53.31 from $75.00, we must again stack our decimal points on top of one another, subtract normally, then bring our decimal point straight down into our answer. The difference of $75.00 and $53.31 is $21.69. So Dave has $21.69 remaining.

## MEASUREMENT EXAMPLES

Mary missed the 1:49 p.m. train. The next train will not arrive until 3:16 p.m. Calculate how much time will pass before the next train arrives. Explain your reasoning.

> Hours are measured in sixty-minute increments. Therefore, to calculate elapsed time we must develop strategies that differ from strategies used with our base-ten number system. The easiest way to calculate the elapsed time between 1:49 p.m. and 3:16 p.m. is to start by determining how many full hours will occur between

them. One full hour past 1:49 is 2:49. If we continue with two full hours we arrive at 3:49, which is *after* 3:16. This tells us that only one full hour will elapse between 1:49 and 3:16. After that one full hour has elapsed, it will be 2:49. To determine how much time will pass between 2:49 and 3:16, we can use the 3:00 hour as a benchmark. To start, we can calculate that 11 minutes will pass between 2:49 and 3:00. From there, another 16 minutes will pass between 3:00 and 3:16. When we add 11 and 16, we have a total of 27 minutes. This tells us that one full hour, 60 minutes, plus 27 more minutes will elapse between 1:49 and 3:16. The total amount of elapsed time is 87 minutes, or 1 hour and 27 minutes.

Jennie measured 38 grams of flour into a bowl. When she placed the bowl on a scale, the measurement read 104 grams. Discuss what Jennie can conclude about the mass of the bowl.

When Jennie placed the bowl on the scale, her measurement was greater than the amount of flour she placed *inside* the bowl. If Jennie knows that the flour accounts for 38 grams of her new weight, she can use subtraction to find the mass of the bowl. She can do this by subtracting the weight of the flour, 38 grams, from the total weight on the scale, 104 grams. The difference of 104 and 38 is 66. Jennie can conclude that the weight, or mass, of the bowl is 66 grams.

A piece of string measures 5 inches. Calculate how long the string measures in centimeters. Round your answer to the nearest whole centimeter and explain your process.

To start, we must use the conversion rate that one inch is equivalent to 2.54 centimeters. If the string is 5 inches long, we must multiply 5 by 2.54 to find the length of the string in centimeters. The product of 5 and 2.54 is 12.7 centimeters. Next, we must round our product to the nearest whole centimeter. To determine our rule for rounding to the nearest whole number, we must look at the digit in the tenths place, the 7. Since 7 is greater than 5, we know to round up, or in other words, to increase the ones place by one whole. That makes 12.7 rounded to the nearest whole number, 13. Our 5-inch string is approximately 13 centimeters long.

John would like to treat his staff of 30 employees to a catered lunch. The catering company charges $15.00 per person. John estimates the lunch will cost him $45.00. Explain and correct John's error.

John made an error using the mental math trick of taking away, then reinserting zeros when multiplying by large numbers ending in zero. To mentally calculate 30 times 15, we can ignore the zero (for a moment), and simply multiply 3 times 15, which equals 45. However, we must now replace the zero we ignored, turning 45 into 450. John forgot to replace the zero he omitted when he applied his mental math trick. Therefore, John can expect to pay $450.00 for his catered lunch of thirty employees, not $45.00.

## PERIMETER VS. AREA OF TWO-DIMENSIONAL FIGURES

The perimeter of a two-dimensional figure is the measure *around* the figure. In other words, the perimeter is the total distance of all the edges making up the figure. For two-dimensional shapes, we find the perimeter by finding the sum of an object's side lengths. In real life, we could use the perimeter to determine how much fencing we would need to enclose a yard or dog pen. Area, on the other hand, measures the surface of two-dimensional figures. We can also think of area as the measure used to determine how many square units would fit within the two-dimensional object. The formula to calculate area varies depending on the shape. For example, multiplying the base and height, then dividing that product by two, calculates the area of any triangle. The area of a square, however, is found simply by multiplying the base and height. In real-life, we calculate the area when we are determining how many tiles we need to re-tile a kitchen floor, or how much seed is needed to cover a portion of land.

## PERIMETER AND AREA EXAMPLES

A rectangular closet measures 6 feet by 8 feet. New carpet costs $2.50 per square foot. Calculate the cost to re-carpet the closet. Explain your process.

> In order to calculate the cost of re-carpeting the closet, we must first calculate the area of the closet. To find the area of any rectangle, we can multiply its length by its width. Here, we have a 6-foot by 8-foot closet. Since the product of 6 and 8 is 48, we know the area of the closet is 48 square feet. Next, we must determine the cost of re-carpeting the closet. To calculate this, we multiply the area of the closet by the cost of the carpet per square foot. If the area of the closet is 48 square feet, and carpet costs $2.50 per square foot, we must find the product of 48 and $2.50, which is $120.00. Therefore, it will cost $120.00 to re-carpet the closet.

The perimeter of a rectangle is 58 feet, with a length of 20 feet. Find the width of the rectangle and explain your process.

> To find the perimeter of any rectangle we must find the sum of its side lengths. We can think of this formula as Perimeter = length + length + width + width. We are given the perimeter and length of the rectangle, which allows us to rewrite our equation as 58 = 20 + 20 + width + width. Once simplified we have the equation 58 = 40 + 2w, or more algebraically, 58 = 2w + 40. To solve for our missing width, we must isolate the variable by performing the inverse operations of those included in the equation. We must start by subtracting 40 from both sides of the equation, which simplifies to 18 = 2w. Next, we can divide both sides of the equation by 2, which leaves us with 9 = w. The width of the rectangle is 9 feet. We can check our answer by inserting 9 into our original equation, 50 = 2(9) + 40. Since the product of 2 and 9 is 18, and 18 + 40 equals 58, we know we are correct.

The area of a trapezoid is 40 square feet, with a height of 5 feet. Prove what you can conclude about the sum of its bases. Justify your answer.

> To find the area of any trapezoid we must follow the formula $A = \frac{1}{2}h(b_1 + b_2)$, where $h$ represents the height and $b$ represents each base of the trapezoid. Here, we are given the area and height of the trapezoid, allowing us to rewrite the equation as $40 = \frac{1}{2} \times 5 \times (b_1 + b_2)$. When simplified, we have $40 = 2.5 \times (b_1 + b_2)$. We can use inverse operations to simplify our equation further by dividing both sides of the equation by 2.5. This leaves us with $16 = (b_1 + b_2)$. We do not have enough information to simplify our equation further, however we can conclude that the sum

30

of the trapezoid's bases must be equivalent to 16 feet since we have proven that $b_1 + b_2$ must equal 16.

---

**Review Video: How to Find the Area and Perimeter**
Visit mometrix.com/academy and enter code: 471797

---

## USING REPEATED ADDITION TO CALCULATE THE AREA OF A RECTANGULAR ARRAY

Rectangular arrays are comprised of identical rows, stacked on top of one another to model the multiplication of two numbers. For example, drawing four rows, each of which contain six identical objects placed directly on top of one another can represent the product of 4 and 6. To calculate the area of that rectangular array, we can simply skip count by 4's, six times. The act of skip-counting is in essence repeatedly adding four to the previous term. In this example, our repeated addition would result in the sequence 4, 8, 12, 16, 20, 24. Using the strategy of repeated addition, we could use our rectangular array to conclude that the product of 4 and 6 is 24.

## REPEATED ADDITION EXAMPLE

Randy has 30 large foam squares to create a play area outside. Determine how many different ways Randy can arrange his squares to create a rectangular play area.

> To form a rectangular array, we must arrange our squares into rows that contain an equal number of squares. The easiest way to approach this type of problem is to list the factor pairs of 30. The first factor pair of any number is 1 and itself. That makes our first option to create 1 row of 30 squares, or 30 rows of 1 square. The number 30 is divisible by 2, making our next factor pair 2 and 15. This means our next option is to create 15 rows of 2 squares, or 2 rows of 15 squares. Thirty is also divisible by 3, which leads us to our next possible arrangement, 3 rows of 10 squares, or 10 rows of 3 squares. Since 30 is not divisible by 4, we can move on to our final factor pair of 5 and 6. Our last option is to create 5 rows of 6 squares, or 6 rows of 5 squares. Moving forward, we would only repeat all of the factor pairs that we have already discovered, so we can conclude that 30 has four factor pairs, providing Randy with eight different options for arranging the squares.

## METRIC EXAMPLES

Identify which metric unit would be the best choice for measuring the length of your thumb. Justify your reasoning.

> The four most common units used to measure length in the metric system are millimeters, centimeters, meters, and kilometers. When deciding on units of measurement, it is helpful to have common objects that you can compare each unit to, in order to visualize the size of each unit. A millimeter is approximately the width of a pencil point. A centimeter is approximately the length of a staple, while a meter is similar to the width of a standard doorway. Kilometers are typically used to measure distance, with each kilometer measuring a bit longer than half a mile. To measure your thumb, centimeters would be the most appropriate metric unit to use. Millimeters would prove too small for efficient measuring, while meters and kilometers would prove much too large.

Assess how the weight of a one-kilogram object relates to a one-gram object. Give an example of an object that might weigh one kilogram and an object that might weigh one gram.

The prefix kilo- implies multiplication by 1,000. It makes sense that within the metric system, the prefix kilo- is used to represent one thousand grams, meters, or liters. For measurements involving weight, one kilogram is equal to 1,000 grams. Therefore, an object weighing one kilogram would be one thousand times heavier than an object weighing one gram. We can think of objects to help us make sense of these weights. For example, a paper clip weighs approximately one gram, while a pineapple is about 1,000 times heavier than that, weighing approximately one kilogram.

## RELATIONSHIP BETWEEN KILOLITERS, LITERS, AND MILLILITERS

In the metric system, liters are used to measure capacity. A kiloliter holds 1,000 liters, while a liter holds 1,000 milliliters. When trying to make sense of the metric system, it helps to have objects that we can relate and envision for each measurement. We can think of a kiloliter as the amount of water needed to fill a small baby pool. On a smaller scale, a large Gatorade bottle holds one liter of liquid, while a single drop of liquid from a medicine dropper is approximately one milliliter.

## DATA COLLECTION

### RELATIONSHIP BETWEEN A SAMPLE AND A POPULATION DURING DATA COLLECTION

In statistics, the term "population" is used to describe the entire group that we are collecting information about. In most cases, it is nearly impossible to collect data on every single member of that population, so samples are formed. A "sample" refers to a subset of a larger population, used to analyze and make assumptions about the population as a whole. For example, if we wanted to find out the favorite ice-cream flavor of sixth graders in New Jersey, we would have to survey a sample of sixth graders, since asking every single sixth-grader is not feasible. To be sure our sample represents the differences within that population, we would have to collect data from all parts of that population, meaning we would ask sixth-graders across the entire state of New Jersey. From our sample, we can make assumptions about the favorite ice-cream flavor of sixth-graders across New Jersey as a population.

### FREQUENCY TABLES

When collecting data from a sample, data can become unorganized and difficult to make sense of. Using frequency tables helps us to organize our data as it is being collected. Let's say we are asking car salesmen how many cars, on average, they sell in a month. Rather than have a random, disorganized list of their responses (such as 4, 6, 2, 4, 1, etc.), we can create a frequency table to use as we collect our data. This would look like a T-chart, where the number of cars is listed in ascending order on the left side, and the frequency of each response is represented using tally marks on the right side. For example, our list of numbers on the left side of the frequency table might be the numbers 0-10. On the right side of the frequency table would be tally marks representing the number of times each response was collected. If four salesmen respond that they sell six cars a month, there would be four tally marks next to the number 6. Using a frequency table while collecting data keeps our data organized, thus making it easy to compare our data at a glance.

## REPRESENTING DATA EXAMPLE

A teacher surveys her class, asking them to identify their favorite day of the week. List three different ways the teacher can represent her data.

> The teacher has collected categorical data, meaning her responses are all grouped into specific categories. Here, her categories are represented by the days of the week (Monday, Tuesday, Wednesday, etc.). The teacher can represent her data in several ways. One option is a dot plot. To create a dot plot, she would need to draw a

32

horizontal axis, with each of the days of the week listed below the line. Each student's response would be represented by a single dot over the day each student chose as his or her favorite. The teacher can also choose to create a bar graph to display her data, in which she would list the days of the week along the x-axis and the frequency of each response along the y-axis. The number of times each day was reported as a student's favorite would be represented by the height of the bar above that category. A third way the teacher could represent her data is by creating a pie chart in which different portions (or slices) of a circle would represent the different percentages that each day of the week was chosen as a student's favorite.

> **Review Video: Data Interpretation of Graphs**
> Visit mometrix.com/academy and enter code: 200439

## USING A BAR GRAPH TO DETERMINE THE NUMBER OF PEOPLE SURVEYED

When analyzing a bar graph, the height of each bar is used to display the frequency in which each category was recorded as a response. We can use a bar graph to find the total number of people surveyed by determining the number of people represented in each bar, and then finding the sum of those values. For example, in a bar graph that includes five categories, we can determine the height, otherwise known as the frequency, of each bar. If the heights of each bar show frequencies of 10, 12, 8, 16, and 9, we can find the sum of those numbers to find the total number of people surveyed. In this example, the sum of 10, 12, 8, 16, and 9 is 55, which tells us that 55 total people were surveyed.

## FINDING THE MODE OF A DATA SET IN A LINE PLOT

The mode of a data set represents the piece of data that is most common, or the most frequently collected piece of data. For example, if we asked a school full of students to identify their favorite subject, the subject chosen most often would be considered the mode of the data set. On a line plot, we can find the mode by looking for the category with the tallest set of dots. On a line plot, the mode is also referred to as the "peak." At times, there is more than one mode (or peak) of a data set. This occurs when two or more categories are tied for having the most pieces of data, or equally tall groups of dots. In this case, we would identify all of the modes. On the other hand, if data is equally represented, with no piece of data occurring more than any other piece of data, we would simply say there is "no mode."

## BAR GRAPHS VS. HISTOGRAMS

The most important difference between bar graphs and histograms is the way in which they group their categories. Bar graphs have only one piece of data per category, while histograms are used when intervals are needed to graph numeric data. Let's suppose we ask teenagers how many times a month they eat pizza. Our responses would be quite diverse, compelling us to group our data into intervals such as 0-4, 5-9, 10-14, etc. This type of grouping would force us to visually represent our data using a histogram, not a bar graph. With histograms, all of our pieces of data between each interval are included in the appropriate bar. This makes it impossible to find statistical measures using a histogram, since we do not know the individual pieces of data being represented, but rather a summary of that data's intervals. Another way bar graphs and histograms differ in found in the way the actual bars are drawn on the graph. The bars on a bar graph have gaps between them, while the bars of a histogram are adjacent to one another, with the exception of intervals containing no data.

# Social Studies

## Social Studies Foundations

### HUMAN SOCIALIZATION AND MAJOR SOCIALIZING AGENCIES

Socialization is the process by which individuals learn their society's norms, values, beliefs, and attitudes; and what behaviors society expects of them relative to those parameters. This learning is imparted by agencies of socialization. The family, peer groups, and leaders of opinion are considered primary socializing agencies. The family is probably the most important because it has the most significant influence on individual development. Families influence the self-concept, feelings, attitudes, and behaviors of each individual member. As children grow, they encounter peer groups throughout life, which also establish norms and values to which individual group members conform. Schools, workplaces, religions, and mass media are considered secondary socializing agencies. Schools dictate additional academic and behavioral norms, values, beliefs, and behaviors. Workplaces have their own cultures that continue, modify, and/or add to the values and behaviors expected of their members. Religions also regulate members' behavior through beliefs, values, goals, and norms that reflect moral principles within a society. Mass media communicate societal conventions (e.g., fashion/style), which enables individuals to learn and adopt new behaviors and/or lifestyles.

### INFLUENCE OF INSTITUTIONS ON THE DEVELOPMENT OF INDIVIDUAL IDENTITY, RELATIONSHIPS, BELIEFS, AND BEHAVIORS

Family is the first and most important socializing agent. Infants learn behavioral patterns from mothers. Their primary socialization is enabled through such early behaviors as nursing, smiling, and toddling. Babies soon interact with other family members. All the infant's physiological and psychological needs are met within the family. Babies learn their sleeping, eating, and toileting habits within the family environment. Babies' personalities also develop based on their early experiences, especially the amounts and types of parental love and affection they receive. School is also a critical socializing agent. Children extend family relationships to society when they go to school. Cognitive and social school experiences develop children's knowledge, skills, beliefs, interests, attitudes, and customs, and help determine the roles children will play when they become adults. In addition to family relationships, receiving reinforcements at school and observing and imitating teachers influence personality development. Peer groups that are based on friendships, shared ideas, and common interests in music, sports, etc. teach children/teens about conforming to rules and being rejected for not complying with these rules. Mass media like TV profoundly influence children, both negatively and positively.

### CULTURE

While no single definition of culture is universally embraced, one from the cultural anthropology perspective is "...a system of shared beliefs, values, customs, behaviors and artifacts that members of society use to cope with their worlds and with one another, and that are transmitted from generation to generation through learning." (Bates and Fratkin, 2002) Cultural groups are based on a wide range of factors, including geographic location, occupation, religion, sexual orientation, income, etc. Individuals may follow the beliefs and values of more than one culture concurrently. For instance, recent immigrants often espouse values and beliefs from both their original and adopted countries. Traditionally, social systems like education and healthcare have approached cultural diversity by focusing on race/ethnicity and common beliefs about various racial/ethnic group customs. These are frequently generalizations (e.g., lumping Mexican, Cuban, and Puerto

34

Rican cultures together and describing them as "Latino" culture). This type of practice can lead to oversimplified stereotypes, and therefore to unrealistic behavioral expectations. Service professionals need more detailed knowledge of cultural complexities and subtleties to effectively engage and interact with families.

## COLLECTIVISM AND INDIVIDUALISM

Certain world cultures are oriented more toward collectivism, while others are oriented more toward individualism. Native American, Latin American, Asian, and African cultures are more often collectivistic, focusing on interdependence, social interactions, relationships, and connections among individuals. North American, Canadian, European, and Australian cultures are more commonly individualistic, focusing on independence, uniqueness, self-determination, and self-actualization (realizing one's full potential). Individualism favors competition and distinguishing oneself as an individual, while collectivism favors cooperation that promotes and contributes to the harmony and well-being of the group. Individualist cultures value teaching young children object manipulation and scientific thinking, while collectivist cultures value social and relational behaviors. For example, adults in collectivist cultures may interpret a child's first steps as walking toward the adult, while adults in individualist cultures interpret them as developing motor skills and autonomy. These interpretations signify what each culture values most, forming the child's cultural orientation early in life. The planning and design of educational and other programs should be informed by a knowledge of these and other cultural differences.

## CULTURAL COMPETENCE

### CULTURALLY COMPETENT PROFESSIONALS

A culturally competent professional demonstrates the ability to enable "...mutually rewarding interactions and meaningful relationships in the delivery of effective services for children and family whose cultural heritage differs from his or her own." (Shonkoff, National Research Council and Institute of Medicine, 2000) Providing interpreters and/or translators does not on its own constitute cultural competence. Hiring racially diverse educational staff in schools is also not enough. Culturally competent educators demonstrate highly developed self-awareness of their own cultural values and beliefs. They must also have and/or develop communication skills that allow them to elicit information from students and families regarding their own cultural beliefs. Further, they must be able to understand how diverse cultural views may affect a child's education, as well as how parents/families receive, comprehend, interpret, and respond to educators' communications. Therefore, educators must develop communication skills to meet educational goals.

### ASPECTS OF CULTURAL COMPETENCE

It is important for educational professionals to acquire and demonstrate cultural competence at the individual level to effectively interact with individual children and their families. Moreover, cultural competence is also important at the program level, the school level, and the system level. According to the National Center for Cultural Competence (NCCC), system level cultural competence is a continuing process that includes "...valuing diversity, conducting self-assessments (including organizational assessments), managing the dynamics of differences, acquiring and institutionalizing cultural knowledge, and adapting to the diversity and cultural contexts of the individuals and communities served." (Goode, 2001) Individual educational interactions are informed by a knowledge of cultural diversity and of the importance of such diversity in educational settings, an ability to adapt to the population's cultural needs, and a willingness to engage in ongoing self-reflection. This same set of knowledge and skills is also applied at the system level. Family engagement is important in EC care and education. This includes understanding the developmental needs of families as well as their children, especially when families and/or children speak different languages.

## ACCULTURATION VERSUS ASSIMILATION

Acculturation describes the process whereby people adapt or change their cultural traditions, values, and beliefs as a result of coming into contact with and being influenced by other cultures over time. Some cultures adopt certain characteristics from other cultures they are exposed to, and two or more separate cultures may sometimes virtually fuse. However, assimilation, wherein various ethnic groups unite to form a new culture, is different from acculturation. One dominant culture may assimilate others. A historical example is the Roman Empire, which forced many members of ancient Greek, Hebrew, and other cultures to abandon their own cultures and adopt Roman law, military allegiance, traditions, language, religion, practices, and customs (including dress). The extent of a diverse cultural group's acculturation influences how it interacts with social systems like education and healthcare. Groups that are strongly motivated to maintain their cultural identity may interact less with mainstream systems that significantly conflict with or vary from their own cultural beliefs.

## MEASURING THE ACCULTURATION OF IMMIGRANTS AND DIVERSE CULTURAL GROUPS IN AMERICA

Social scientists currently use indices such as people's country of birth, how long they have lived in America, their knowledge of the English language, and their level of English language use to study acculturation. However, these factors are measured not because they are the core elements of acculturation, but because they are easier to validly and reliably measure than the underlying cultural beliefs, attitudes, and behaviors they reflect, which are harder to quantify. The interactions between American educators and culturally diverse families can be problematic on both sides. Educators have difficulty interacting, communicating, and collaborating with families that come from a variety of other countries, speak various other languages, and differ in their degree of acculturation to American culture. On the other hand, immigrant and culturally diverse families encounter a foreign language, different cultural customs and practices, and an unfamiliar educational system with different methods of assessment, placement, curriculum planning and design, instruction, and evaluation—not to mention different special education laws and procedures. Thus, the acculturation challenges related to interactions between American educators and culturally diverse families are bilateral.

## CULTURAL DIFFERENCES IN PARENTS' GOALS FOR RAISING THEIR CHILDREN

Depending on their cultural group, parents have varying goals for their children, and use different practices to achieve those goals. For example, research on four different cultural groups in Hawaii found the following differences related to what parents visualized when they pictured their children as successful adults: Native Hawaiians most wanted their children to have social connections, be happy in their social networks, and demonstrate self-reliance as adults. Caucasian American parents most valued self-reliance, happiness, spontaneity, and creativity as developmental outcomes for their children. Filipino American parents most valued the development of traits related to obedience, citizenship, respect for authority, and good conduct and manners in their children. Japanese American parents placed priority on their children's achievement, as well as their ability to live well-organized lives, stay in contact with family, and master the demands of life. Such distinct, significant differences imply that these parent groups would vary in how they would respond to young children's assertive behaviors, in their disciplinary styles (e.g., permissive, authoritative, authoritarian), and in the emphasis they would place on activities focusing on physical and cognitive skill mastery vs. social competence and connection.

## EDUCATIONAL SERVICES ACCESSED BY DIFFERENT CULTURES

Parents in America have been found to show distinct preferences for the kinds of care and educational services they access for their children. For example, Caucasian parents in America are more likely to turn to preschool centers for help with their young children's care and instruction. This preference is influenced not only by custom, but also by scientific evidence that center-based preschool experience improves children's skills and prepares them for school. Hispanic parents in America are more likely to use home-based and/or family-based care settings. This preference probably reflects the more collectivist Hispanic perspective, which places more importance on social relationships than on structured learning in early childhood. Educators can take a culturally competent approach to such cultural diversity by looking for ways in which young children's school readiness skills can be promoted in family and home-based child care settings.

## DIFFERENT VIEWS ON CARE, EDUCATION, AND THE NATURE OF THEIR COGNITIVE ABILITIES

Depending on their native culture, parents vary in terms of the early experiences they select for their young children. For example, Latino parents tend to prefer family-based/home-based care. White parents tend to prefer center-based daycare and education designed to promote school readiness. Another cultural difference is parental beliefs about children's learning capacities. For example, research in California found that the majority of Latino parents believed their children's learning capacity is set at birth; only a small minority of white parents held this belief. Parents subscribing to a transactional child development model view the complex interaction between child and environment as creating a dynamic developmental process. These parents are more likely to value the stimulation of early childhood development, seek/implement activities that will provide such stimulation, and access early intervention services for children with developmental delays/difficulties. Parents subscribing to a view of fixed, innate cognitive capacity are less likely to believe their children's cognitive abilities can be influenced by educational experiences, and may not see the benefits of or seek out early learning stimulation and intervention.

## CULTURAL AND OTHER INFLUENCES AND HOW MUCH PARENTS IN AMERICA READ TO THEIR CHILDREN

Researchers analyzing national early childhood surveys have identified significant variations in how often white, Asian, and Hispanic parents read to their young children. This variation is not solely due to varying cultural values. Additional factors include parents' financial limitations; time limitations; familiarity and comfort with accessing libraries and other government resources, websites, etc.; and literacy levels in both English and their native languages. Educators must realize that trying to encourage or even teach parents to read to their children earlier and/or more often is unlikely to be successful if parents do not place value or priority on the benefits of being read to, or do not view the outcomes of reading aloud to children as benefits. Reading to children is known to promote school readiness and academic success. Educators should also understand that some children, despite not being read to in early childhood, become successful adults. Additionally, some cultures, including African Americans, emphasize oral learning traditions more than written ones, developing different skills, such as the basic understanding of story flow.

## FACTORS AFFECTING PARENTS WHO ARE IMMIGRANTS TO AMERICA

Parents educated in other countries may not know a great deal about the American educational system, and may not be aware of the educational demands made on their children, even in early childhood. Educators need to work with these parents to find common ground by identifying shared goals for children. While culturally diverse parents may disagree with some educators' goals, they can collaborate with educators to promote those on which they do agree. Immigrant parents may also be unaware of additional services available in America for children with developmental and/or learning problems. Educators can help parents by providing this information. Another consideration is that some other cultures have more paternalistic educational systems. Parents from such cultures, rather than vocally advocating for their children who need services, tend to wait for teachers/specialists to voice concerns before communicating any problems they have observed. Thus, they could miss out on the chance to obtain helpful services. Even worse, educators could misconstrue their behavior as a lack of interest in children's progress, or as resistance to confronting problems.

## DEVELOPMENTAL MILESTONES VARYING BY CULTURE

Research has found that different cultures have different age expectations for many early childhood developmental milestones. For example, Filipinos expect children to eat using utensils at 32.4 months. Anglo families expect children to do this at 17.7 months, and Puerto Ricans expect children to reach this milestone at 26.5 months. Filipino cultures expect children to sleep all night by 32.4 months; Puerto Rican and Anglo cultures expect this at 14.5 and 14.4 months, respectively. Similarly, while Anglos expect children to sleep by themselves at around 13.8 months and Puerto Ricans at around 14.6 months, Filipinos do not expect this until 38.8 months. Filipinos expect children to eat solid food by 6.7 months; Anglos by 8.2 months; and Puerto Ricans by 10.1 months. In Anglo families, an 18-month-old not drinking from a cup could indicate developmental delay if parents introduced the cup when s/he was one year old and regularly continued encouraging cup use. But, Filipino parents of an 18-month-old have likely not even introduced the child to a cup yet, so the fact that the child is not using a cup would not be cause for concern from a development standpoint.

When EC researchers investigated the average expectations of different cultural groups of when children would reach various developmental milestones, some of the milestones they examined included: eating solid food, weaning from nursing, drinking from a cup, eating with the fingers, eating with utensils, sleeping alone, sleeping through the night, choosing one's own clothes, dressing oneself, and playing alone. They also looked at daytime and nighttime toilet training. Educators must become aware of different cultures' different socialization goals before assuming culturally diverse children have developmental delays. On the other hand, they must also avoid automatically attributing variations in milestone achievement to cultural child rearing differences when full developmental assessments might be indicated. Family expectations and values influence the complex process of developmental assessment. When families and assessors share common cultures, it is more likely that valid data will be collected and interpreted. When their cultures differ, however, it is more likely that the assessment information will be misinterpreted. Employing EC teachers/care providers who are familiar with the child, family, and assessment setting as mediators can make developmental assessments more culturally competent.

## ESSENTIAL GEOGRAPHICAL CONCEPTS

Ten concepts considered essential to the study of geography are: location, distance, achievability, pattern, morphology, agglomeration, utility value, interaction, area differentiation, and spatial interrelatedness. (1) Location: This concept identifies "where" a place is and examines the positive and negative properties of any place on the surface of the Earth. Absolute location is based upon latitude and longitude. Relative location is based upon changing characteristics of a region, and is influenced by surrounding areas. For example, urban areas have higher land prices than rural ones. (2) Distance: This identifies "how far" a place is, and is often described in terms of location. It is also related to the effort required to meet basic life needs. For example, the distance of raw materials from factories affects transportation costs and hence product prices. In another example, land costs less the farther it is from highways. (3) Achievability: The conditions on the Earth's surface dictate how accessible a geographic area is. For example, villages on beaches are easier to reach. Villages

38

surrounded by forests or swamps are harder to reach. As its economy, science, technology, and transportation develop, a region's level of dependency on other areas changes.

(4) Patterns These are found in geographical forms and in how geographical phenomena spread, which affect dependency on those phenomena. For example, in fold regions (areas where the folding of rocks forms mountains), the rivers typically form trellis patterns. Patterns are also seen in human activity that is based on geography. For example, in mountainous regions, settlements predominantly form spreading patterns. (5) Morphology This is the shape of our planet's surface resulting from inner and outer forces. For example, along the northern coast of Java, sugarcane plantations predominate on the lowlands. (6) Agglomeration This is defined as collecting into a mass, and refers to a geographic concentration of people, activities, and/or settlements within areas that are most profitable and relatively narrow in size. (7) Utility value This refers to the existence and relative usefulness of natural resources. For example, fishermen find more utility value in the ocean than farmers do, and naturalists perceive more utility value in forests than academics would.

(8) Interaction This is the reciprocal and interdependent relationship between two or more geographical areas, which can generate new geographical phenomena, configurations, and problems. For example, a rural village produces raw materials through activities like mining ores or growing and harvesting plant crops, while a city produces industrial goods. The village needs the city as a market for its raw materials, and may also need the city's industrial products. The city needs the village for its raw materials to use in industrial production. This interdependence causes interaction. (9) Area differentiation This informs the study of variations among regional geographical phenomena. For example, different plants are cultivated in highlands vs. lowlands due to their different altitudes and climates. Area differentiation also informs the study of regional variations in occupation (farming vs. fishing, etc.). (10) Spatial interrelatedness This shows the relationship between/among geographic and non-physical phenomena, like rural and urban areas. The example above of village-city interaction also applies here.

## GEOGRAPHICAL MAPS
### GENERAL FEATURES AND PURPOSES
Maps can be drawn to show natural or man-made features. For example, some maps depict mountains, elevations (altitudes), average rainfall, average temperatures, and other natural features of an area. Other maps are made to depict countries, states, cities, roads, empires, wars, and other man-made features. Some maps include both natural and man-made features (e.g., a map showing a certain country and its elevations). Different types of maps are described according to their purposes. For example, political maps are made to depict countries, areas within a country, and/or cities. Physical maps are drawn to display natural features of the terrain in an area, such as rivers, lakes, and mountains. Thematic maps are drawn to focus on a more specific theme or topic, such as the locations and names of battles during a war or the average amounts of rainfall a country, state, or region receives in a given year or month. Some maps are made for more than one purpose, and indicate more than one of the types of information described above.

### BASIC TOOLS SUPPLIED ON MAPS
On maps depicting local, national, and world geography, cartographers supply tools for navigating these maps. For example, the compass rose indicates the directions of north, south, east, and west. By looking at the compass, people can identify the locational relationships of places (e.g., in South America, Chile is west of Argentina). The scale of miles indicates how distances on a map correspond to actual geographical distances, enabling us to estimate real distances. For example, the scale might show that one inch is equal to 500 miles. By placing a piece of paper on the map, we

can mark it to measure the distance between two cities (e.g., Washington, DC, in the USA and Ottawa in Canada) on the map, and then line the paper up with the scale of miles to estimate an actual distance of approximately 650 miles between the two cities. Map keys/legends identify what a map's symbols and colors represent.

## GRIDS

Maps show absolute geographic location (i.e. the precise "address" of any place on the planet) using a grid of lines. The lines running from east to west are called parallels or latitudes, and they correspond to how many degrees away from the equator a place is located. The lines running from north to south are called meridians or longitudes, and they correspond to how many degrees away from the prime meridian a place is located. To determine the absolute location of a place, we find the spot on the map where its latitude and longitude intersect. This intersection is the place's absolute location. For example, if we look at Mexico City on a map, we will find that its latitude is 19° north and its longitude is 99° west, which is expressed in cartography as 19° N, 99° W. Numbers of latitudes and longitudes like these are also referred to as coordinates.

## READING AND ANALYZING A SPECIAL PURPOSE MAP

(1) First, read a map's title and look at the overall map. This provides a general idea of what the map shows. For example, a map entitled "Battles of the Punic Wars" would not be a good choice if someone was looking for the political boundaries of modern day Greece, Italy, and Spain. (2) Next, read the map's legend/key to see what symbols and colors the map uses, and what each represents. For example, some lines represent divisions between countries/states; some, roads; some, rivers; etc. Different colors can indicate different countries/states, elevations, amounts of rainfall, population densities, etc. These are not uniform across all maps, so legends/keys are necessary references. (3) Use the legend/key to interpret what the map shows. For example, by looking at colors representing elevations, one can determine which area of a country has the highest/lowest altitude. (4) Draw conclusions about what the map displays. For example, if a country map mainly has one color that indicates a certain elevation range, it can be concluded that this is the country's most common elevation.

## GRAPHS

Graphs display numerical information in pictorial forms, making it easier to view statistics quickly and draw conclusions about them. For example, it is easier to see patterns/trends like increases/decreases in quantities using visual graphs than columns of numbers. Line graphs, bar graphs, and pie charts are the most common types of graphs. Line graphs depict changes over time by plotting points for a quantity measured each day/week/month/year/decade/century etc. and connecting the points to make a line. For example, showing the population of a city/country each decade in a line graph reveals how the population has risen/fallen/both. Bar graphs compare quantities related to different times/places/people/things. Each quantity is depicted by a separate bar, and its height/length corresponds to a number. Bar graphs make it easy to see which amounts are largest/smallest within a group (e.g., which of several cities/countries has the largest population). Pie charts/circle graphs divide a circle/"pie" into segments/"slices" showing percentages/parts of a whole, which also facilitates making comparisons. For example, the city/country with the largest population is the largest segment on a pie chart or circle graph.

> **Review Video: Data Interpretation of Graphs**
> Visit mometrix.com/academy and enter code: 200439
>
> **Review Video: Identifying Units and Trends in a Chart**
> Visit mometrix.com/academy and enter code: 638347

## IMPORTANCE OF CHRONOLOGICAL THINKING TO UNDERSTANDING HISTORY

To see cause-and-effect relationships in historical events and explore and understand relationships among those events, students must have a solid grasp of when things happened and in what time sequence (chronology). Teachers can help students develop chronological thinking by using and assigning well-constructed/well-written narratives. These include histories written in the same style as stories, works of historical literature, and biographies. These hold students' attention, allowing them to focus on authors' depictions of temporal relationships among antecedents, actions, and consequences; of historical motivations and deeds of individuals and groups; and of the time structure of sequential occurrences. By middle school, students should have the skills needed to measure time mathematically (e.g., in years/decades/centuries/millennia), interpret data displayed in timelines, and calculate time in BC and AD. High school students should be able to analyze patterns of historical duration (e.g., how long the U.S. Constitutional government has lasted) and patterns of historical succession (e.g., the development of expanding trade and communication systems, from Neolithic times through ancient empires and from early modern times to modern global interaction).

## EDUCATIONAL STANDARDS THAT DEMONSTRATE SKILLS IN HISTORICAL AND CHRONOLOGICAL THINKING

Students should be able to differentiate among past, present, and future. They should be able to identify the beginning, middle, and end/outcome of historical narratives/stories. They also should be able to construct their own historical narratives, including working forward and backward in time from some event to explain causes and temporal development of various events, issues, etc. Students should be able to calculate and measure calendar time, including days/dates, weeks, months, years, centuries, and millennia. They should be able to describe time periods using BC and AD They should be skilled at comparing calendar systems (e.g., Roman, Gregorian, Julian, Hebrew, Muslim, Mayan, and others) and at relating the calendar years of major historical events. They should be able to look at timelines and interpret the information they contain, and make their own timelines using equidistant time intervals and recording events sequentially. Students should be able to explain change and continuity in history through reconstructing and applying patterns of historical duration and succession. They should be able to identify the structural principles that are the bases of alternative periodization models, and to compare these models.

## REASONS/PURPOSES FOR OUR COUNTRY'S LAWS AND TEACHING CITIZENSHIP

Young children must understand the purposes of rules/laws: They identify acceptable/unacceptable citizen behaviors; make society and life predictable, secure, and orderly; designate responsibilities to citizens; and prevent persons in authority positions from abusing their roles by limiting their power. Understanding these functions of laws/rules enables children to realize that our government consists of individuals and groups authorized to create, implement, and enforce laws and manage legal disputes. Some creative EC teachers have used children's literature to illustrate these concepts. Children can relate personally to stories' characters, and story situations make the concepts real and concrete to children. Stories can be springboards for discussing rules and when they do/do not apply. One activity involves children in small groups making class rules (e.g., "No talking" and "Stay in your seat"), and then rewriting these to be more realistic (e.g., "Talk softly in class; listen when others talk" and "Sit down and get right to work"). Children consider issues of safety and fairness, and develop an understanding of judicial and legislative roles.

# Science

## Science Foundations

### SCIENCE CONCEPTS YOUNG CHILDREN LEARN DURING EVERYDAY ACTIVITIES

Science entails asking questions, conducting investigations, collecting data, and seeking answers to the questions asked by analyzing the data collected. Natural events that can be examined over time and student-centered inquiry through hands-on activities that require the application of problem solving skills are most appropriate for helping young children learn basic science. In their everyday lives, young children develop concepts of 1:1 correspondence through activities like fitting pegs into matching holes or distributing one item to each child in a class. They also develop counting concepts by counting enough items for each child in the group or counting pennies in a piggy bank. They develop classification concepts when they sort objects into separate piles according to their shapes or some other type of category (e.g., toy cars vs. toy trucks). When children transfer water, sand, rice, or other substances from one container to another, they develop measurement concepts. As they progress, children will apply these early concepts to more abstract scientific ideas during grade school.

### SCIENCE CONCEPTS INFANTS AND TODDLERS LEARN IN NORMAL DEVELOPMENTAL PROCESSES

Infants use their senses to explore the environment, and are motivated by innate curiosity. As they develop mobility, children gain more freedom, allowing them to make independent discoveries and think for themselves. Children learn size concepts by comparing the sizes of objects/persons in the environment to their own size, and by observing that some objects are too large to hold, while others are small enough to hold. They learn about weight when trying to lift various objects. They learn about shape when they see that some objects roll away, while others do not. Babies learn temporal sequences when they wake up wet and hungry, cry, and have parents change and feed them. They also learn this concept by playing, getting tired, and going to sleep. As soon as they look and move around, infants learn about space, including large/small spaces. Eventually, they develop spatial sense through experiences like being put in a playpen/crib in the middle of a large room. Toddlers naturally sort objects into groups according to their sizes/shapes/colors/uses. They experiment with transferring water/sand among containers of various sizes. They learn part-to-whole relationships by building block structures and then dismantling them.

### NATURALISTIC, INFORMAL, AND STRUCTURED LEARNING EXPERIENCES

Children actively construct their knowledge of the environment through exploring it. Young children's learning experiences can be naturalistic (i.e. spontaneously initiated by the child during everyday activities). During naturalistic learning, the child controls his/her choices and actions. Informal learning experiences also allow the child to choose his or her actions and activities, but they include adult intervention at some point during the child's engagement in naturalistic pursuits. In structured learning experiences, the adult chooses the activities and supplies some direction as to how the child should perform the associated actions. One consideration related to EC learning that teachers should keep in mind is that within any class or group of children, there are individual differences in learning styles. Additionally, children from different cultural groups have varying learning styles and approaches. EC teachers can introduce science content in developmentally appropriate ways by keeping these variations in mind.

## NATURALISTIC LEARNING EXPERIENCES

Motivated by novelty and curiosity, young children spontaneously initiate naturalistic experiences during their everyday activities. Infants and toddlers in Piaget's sensorimotor stage learn by exploring the environment through their senses, so adults should provide them with many objects and substances they can see, hear, touch, smell, and taste. Through manipulating and observing concrete objects/substances, preschoolers in Piaget's preoperational stage begin learning concepts that will enable them to perform mental operations later on. Adults should observe children's actions and progress, and should give positive reinforcement in the form of looks, facial expressions, gestures, and/or words encouraging and praising the child's actions. Young children need adult feedback to learn when they are performing the appropriate actions. For example, a toddler/preschooler selects a tool from the toolbox, saying, "This is big!" and the mother responds, "Yes!" A four-year-old sorting toys of various colors into separate containers is another example of a naturalistic experience. A five-year-old who observes while painting that mixing two colors yields a third color is yet another example.

## INFORMAL LEARNING EXPERIENCE

Informal learning experiences involve two main components. First, the child spontaneously initiates naturalistic learning experiences during everyday activities to explore and learn about the environment. Second, the adult takes advantage of opportunities during naturalistic experiences to insert informal learning experiences. Adults do not plan these in advance, but take advantage of opportunities that occur naturally. One way this happens is when a child is on the right track to solve a problem, but needs some encouragement or a hint from the adult. Another way is when the adult spots a "teachable moment" during the child's naturalistic activity, and uses it to reinforce a basic concept. For example, a three-year-old might hold up three fingers, declaring, "I'm six years old." The parent says, "Let's count fingers: one, two, three. You're three years old." Or, a teacher asks a child who has a box of treats if s/he has enough for the whole class, and the child answers, "I don't know." The teacher then responds, "Let's count them together," and helps the child count.

## STRUCTURED LEARNING EXPERIENCES

Naturalistic learning experiences are spontaneously initiated and controlled by children. Informal learning experiences involve unplanned interventions by adults during children's naturalistic experiences, which is when adults offer suitable correction/assistance/support. Structured learning experiences differ in that the adult pre-plans and initiates the activity/lesson, and provides the child with some direction. For example, a teacher who observes a four-year-old's need to practice counting can give the child a pile of toys, and then ask him/her how many there are. To develop size concepts, a teacher can give a small group of children several toys of different sizes, and then ask the children to inspect them and talk about their characteristics. The teacher holds up one toy, instructing children to find one that is bigger/smaller. If a child needs to learn shape concepts, the teacher might introduce a game involving shapes, giving the child instructions on how to play the game. Or, a first grade teacher, recognizing the importance of the concept of classification to the ability to organize scientific information, might ask students to bring in bones to classify during a unit on skeletons.

## KINDERGARTEN ACTIVITY FOR COLLECTING AND ORGANIZING DATA

Preschoolers and kindergarteners continue their earlier practices of exploration to learn new things, and they apply fundamental science concepts to collect and organize data in order to answer questions. To collect data, children must have observation, counting, recording, and organization skills. One activity kindergarteners and teachers enjoy is growing bean sprouts. For example, the teacher can show children two methods: one using glass jars and paper towels saturated with water, the other using cups of dirt. The children add water daily as needed, observe developments, and report to the teacher, who records their observations on a chart. The teacher gives each child a chart that they add information to each day. The children count how many days their beans took to sprout in the glass jars and in the cups of dirt. They then compare their own results for the two methods, and they compare their results to those of their classmates. The children apply concepts of counting, numbers, time, 1:1 correspondence, and comparison of numbers. They also witness the planting and growing process.

## SCIENCE PROCESS SKILLS

Science process skills include observation (using the senses to identify properties of objects/situations), classification (grouping objects/situations according to their common properties), measurement (quantifying physical properties), communication (using observations, classifications, and measurements to report experimental results to others), inference (finding patterns and meaning in experiment results), and prediction (using experimental experience to formulate new hypotheses). Inferences and predictions must be differentiated from objective observations. Classification, measurement, and comparison are basic math concepts which, when applied to science problems, are called process skills. The other science process skills named, as well as defining and controlling variables, are equally necessary to solve both science and math problems. For example, using ramps can help young children learn basic physics concepts. Teachers ask children what would happen if two balls were rolled down a ramp at the same time, if two balls were rolled down a ramp of a different height/length, if two ramps of different heights/lengths were used, etc. In this activity, children apply the scientific concepts of observation, communication, inference, and prediction, as well as the concepts of height, length, counting, speed, distance, and comparison.

## SCIENTIFIC METHOD

Children are born curious, and naturally engage in problem solving to learn. Problem solving and inquiry are natural child behaviors. EC teachers can use these behaviors to promote children's scientific inquiry. Scientific inquiry employs the scientific method. The first step in the method is to ask a question, which is another natural child behavior. Just as adult scientists formulate research questions, the first step of the scientific method for children is asking questions they want to answer. Next, to address a question, both adults and children must form a hypothesis (i.e. an educated guess about what the answer will be). The hypothesis informs and directs the next steps: designing and conducting an experiment to test whether the hypothesis is true or false. With teacher instruction/help, children experiment. For example, they might drop objects of different weights from a height to see when each lands, as Galileo did. Teachers help record outcomes. The next steps are deciding whether the results prove/disprove the hypothesis and reporting the results and conclusions to others.

> **Review Video: The Scientific Method**
> Visit mometrix.com/academy and enter code: 191386

## PHYSICAL SCIENCE AND MATTER

Physical science is the study/science of the physical universe surrounding us. Everything in the universe consists of matter (i.e. anything that has mass and takes up space) or energy (i.e. anything that does not have mass or occupy space, but affects matter and space). Three states of matter are solid, liquid, and gas. Solids preserve their shape even when they are not in a container. Solids have specific, three-dimensional/crystalline atomic structures and specific melting points. Liquids have no independent shape outside of containers, but have specific volumes. Liquid molecules are less cohesive than solid molecules, but more cohesive than gas molecules. Liquids have flow, viscosity (flow resistance), and buoyancy. Liquids can undergo diffusion, osmosis, evaporation, condensation, solution, freezing, and heat conduction and convection. Liquids and gases are both fluids, and share some of the same properties. Gases have no shape, expanding and spreading indefinitely outside of containers. Gases can become liquid/solid through cooling/compression/both. Liquids/solids can become gaseous through heating. Vapor is the gaseous form of a substance that is solid/liquid at lower temperatures. For example, when water is heated it becomes steam, a vapor.

**Review Video: States of Matter**
Visit mometrix.com/academy and enter code: 742449

## LIQUIDS

Of the three states of matter—solid, liquid, and gas—liquids have properties that fall somewhere in between those of solids and gases. The molecules of solids are the most cohesive (i.e. they have the greatest mutual attraction). Gas molecules are the least cohesive, and liquid molecules are in between. Liquids have no definite shape, while solids do. Liquids have a definite volume, whereas gases do not. The cohesion of liquid molecules draws them together, and the molecules below the surface pull surface molecules down, creating surface tension. This property can be observed in containers of water. Liquid molecules are also attracted to other substance's molecules (i.e. adhesion). Surface tension and adhesion combined cause liquids to rise in narrow containers, a property known as capillarity. Liquids are buoyant (i.e. they exert upward force so objects which have more buoyancy than weight float in liquids, while objects which have more weight than buoyancy sink in liquids). Liquids can be made solid by freezing, and can be made gaseous by heating/evaporation. Liquids can diffuse, which means they can mix with other molecules. Liquid diffusion across semi-permeable membranes is known as osmosis.

## SOLIDS

Solids are one of the three forms of matter. The other two are liquids and gases. Solids maintain their shape when they are not inside of containers, whereas liquids and gases acquire the shapes of containers holding them. Containers also prevent liquids and gases from dispersing. Of the three forms of matter, solids have the most cohesive molecules. Solid molecules are most attracted to each other, and solid molecules are held together most strongly. Solid atoms are organized into defined, three-dimensional, lattice-shaped patterns (i.e. they are crystalline in structure). Solids also have specific temperatures at which they melt. Some substances that seem solid, such as plastic, gel, tar, and glass, are actually not true solids. They are amorphous solids because their atoms do not have a crystalline structure, but are amorphous (i.e. the positions of their atoms have no long-range organization). They also have a range of melting temperatures rather than specific melting points.

**Review Video: Amorphous Solids**
Visit mometrix.com/academy and enter code: 121001

**Review Video: Balance of Forces That Make a Solid**
Visit mometrix.com/academy and enter code: 519967

## GASES

Gas, liquid, and solid are the three states of matter. Gases have the least cohesive (i.e. mutually attracted) molecules of the three states of matter, while solids have the most cohesive molecules. Gases do not maintain a defined shape, while solids do. If not contained within a receptacle, gases spread and expand indefinitely. Gases can be elementary or compound. An elementary gas is composed of only one kind of chemical element. At normal temperatures and pressures, 12

45

elementary gases are known: <u>argon</u>*, chlorine, fluorine, <u>helium</u>*, hydrogen, <u>krypton</u>*, <u>neon</u>*, nitrogen, oxygen, ozone, <u>radon</u>*, and <u>xenon</u>*. Compound gases have molecules containing atoms of more than one kind of chemical element. Carbon monoxide (which contains one carbon and one oxygen atom) and ammonia (which contains nitrogen and hydrogen atoms) are common compound gases. Heating gas molecules/atoms charges them electrically, making them ions. Plasma combines positive gas ions and electrons. Some gases are colorless and odorless, while others are not. Some burn with oxygen, while others do not. *<u>Noble/inert gases</u> have single atoms that do not normally form compounds with other elements.

## LIGHT
### REFLECTION AND SCATTERING

When a beam of light hits a smooth surface like a mirror, it bounces back off that surface. This rebounding is reflection. In physics, the law of reflection states that "the angle of incidence equals the angle of reflection." This means that when light is reflected, it always bounces off the surface at the same angle at which it hit that surface. When a beam of light hits a rough rather than a smooth surface, though, it is reflected back at many different angles, not just the angle at which it struck the surface. This reflection at multiple and various angles is scattering. Many objects we commonly use every day have rough surfaces. For example, paper may look smooth to the naked eye, but actually has a rough surface. This property can be observed by viewing paper through a microscope. Because light waves striking paper are reflected in every direction by its rough surface, scattering enables us to read words printed on paper from any viewing angle.

### ABSORPTION

When light strikes a medium, the light wave's frequency is equal or close to the frequency at which the electrons in the medium's atoms can vibrate. These electrons receive the light's energy, making them vibrate. When a medium's atoms hang on tightly to their electrons, the electrons transmit their vibrations to the nucleus of each atom. This makes the atoms move faster and collide with the medium's other atoms. The energy the atoms got from the vibrations is then released as heat. This process is known as absorption of light. Materials that absorb light, such as wood and metal, are opaque. Some materials absorb certain light frequencies but transmit others. For example, glass transmits visible light (and therefore appears transparent to the naked eye), but absorbs ultraviolet frequencies. The sky looks blue because the atmosphere absorbs all colors in the spectrum except blue, which it reflects. Only blue wavelengths/frequencies bounce back to our eyes. This is an example of subtractive color, which we see in paints/dyes and all colored objects/materials. Pigments absorb some frequencies and reflect others.

### REFRACTION

When light moves from one transparent medium to another (e.g., between water and air/vice versa), the light's speed changes, bending the light wave. It bends either away from or toward the normal line, an imaginary straight line running at right angles to the medium's surface. We easily observe this bending when looking at a straw in a glass of water. The straw appears to break/bend at the waterline. The angle of refraction is the amount that the light wave bends. It is determined by how much the medium slows down the light's speed, which is the medium's refraction index. For example, diamonds are much denser and harder than water, and thus have a higher refraction index. They slow down and trap light more than water does. Consequently, diamonds sparkle more than water. Lenses, such as those in eyeglasses and telescopes, rely on the principle of refraction. Curved lenses disperse or concentrate light waves, refracting light as it both enters and exits, thus changing the light's direction. This is how lenses correct (eyeglasses) and enhance (telescopes) our vision.

## MAGNETISM

Magnetism is the property some objects/substances have of attracting other materials. The form of magnetism most familiar to us is certain materials attracting iron. Magnets also attract steel, cobalt, and other materials. Generators supplying power include magnets, as do all electric motors. Loudspeakers and telephones contain magnets. Tape recorders use magnets. The tape they play is magnetized. Magnets are used in compasses to determine the location of north and various corresponding directions. In fact, the planet Earth is itself a giant magnet (which is why compasses point north). Hence, like the Earth, all magnets have two poles: a north/north-seeking pole and a south/south-seeking pole. Opposite poles attract, and like poles repel each other. Magnets do not need to touch to attract/repel each other. A magnet's effective area/range is its magnetic field. All materials have some response to magnetic fields. Magnets make nearby magnetic materials into magnets, a process known as magnetic induction. Materials that line up parallel to magnetic force field lines are paramagnetic, while materials that line up perpendicular to magnetic force field lines are diamagnetic.

### MODERN THEORY OF MAGNETISM AND WHAT SCIENTISTS DO/DO NOT KNOW

Scientists have known about the effects of magnetism for hundreds of years. However, they do not know exactly what magnetism is, or what causes it. French physicist Pierre Weiss proposed a theory of magnetism in the early 20th century that is widely accepted. This theory posits that every magnetic material has groups of molecules—domains—that function as magnets. Until a material is magnetized, its domains have a random arrangement, so one domain's magnetism is cancelled out by another's. When the material comes into a magnetic field—the range/area wherein a magnet is effective—its domains align themselves parallel to the magnetic field's lines of force. As a result, all of their north-seeking/north poles point in the same direction. Removing the magnetic field causes like poles to repel one another as they normally do. In easily magnetized materials, domains revert to random order. In materials that are harder to magnetize, domains lack sufficient force to disassemble, leaving the material magnetized. Later versions of Weiss's theory attribute domain magnetism to spinning electrons.

> **Review Video: Magnets**
> Visit mometrix.com/academy and enter code: 570803

## INSULATION, CONDUCTION, AND THE FLOW OF ELECTRICITY

The smallest units of all matter are atoms. The nuclei of atoms are orbited by negatively charged electrons. Some materials have electrons that are strongly bound to their atoms. These include air, glass, wood, cotton, plastic, and ceramic. Since their atoms rarely release electrons, these materials have little or no ability to conduct electricity, and are known as electrical insulators. Insulators resist/block conduction. Metals and other conductive materials have free electrons that can detach from the atoms and move around. Without the tight binding of insulators, materials with loose electrons enable electric current to flow easily through them. Such materials are called electrical conductors. The movements of their electrons transmit electrical energy. Electricity requires something to make it flow (i.e. a generator). A generator creates a steady flow of electrons by moving a magnet close to a wire, creating a magnetic field to propel electrons. Electricity also requires a conductor (i.e. a medium through which it can move from one place to another).

## MOVEMENT OF ELECTRICAL CURRENTS BY A GENERATOR

Magnetism and electricity are related, and they interact with each other. Generators work by using magnets near conductive wires to produce moving streams of electrons. The agent of movement can range from a hand crank, to a steam engine, to the nuclear fission process. However, all agents of movements operate according to the same principle. A simple analogy is that a generator magnetically pushes electrical current the way a pump pushes water. Just as water pumps apply specific amounts of pressure to specific numbers of water molecules, generator magnets apply specific amounts of "pressure" to specific numbers of electrons. The number of moving electrons in an electrical circuit equals the current, or amperage. The unit of measurement for amperage is the ampere, or amp. The amount of force moving the electrons is the voltage. Its unit of measurement is the volt. One amp equals $6.24 \times 10^{18}$ electrons passing through a wire each second. For example, a generator could produce 1 amp using 6 volts when rotating 1,000 times per minute. Today's power stations rely on generators.

## POSITIONS AND MOTIONS OF OBJECTS AND NEWTON'S LAWS OF PHYSICS

Moving physical objects changes their positions. According to Newton's first law of motion, an object at rest tends to stay at rest and an object in motion tends to stay in motion, unless/until an opposing force changes the object's state of rest/motion. For example, an object at rest could be a small rock sitting on the ground. If you kick the rock into the air, it moves through the air. The rock will continue to move, but when a force like gravity acts on it, it falls/stops moving. The resulting motion from kicking the rock illustrates Newton's third law of motion: for every action there is an equal and opposite reaction. The acceleration or increase in velocity (a) of an object depends on its mass (m) and the amount of force (F) that is applied to the object. Newton's second law of motion states that F = ma (force equals mass times acceleration). Thus, moving objects maintain their speeds unless some force(s) cause acceleration or slowing/stopping, as frictional forces do.

## HEAT

Heat is transmitted through conduction, radiation, and convection. Heat is transmitted in solids through conduction. When two objects at different temperatures touch each other, the hotter object's molecules are moving faster. They collide with the colder object's molecules, which are moving slower. As a result of the collision, the molecules that are moving more rapidly supply energy to the molecules that are moving more slowly. This speeds up the movement of the (previously) slower moving molecules, which heats up the colder object. This process of transferring heat through contact is called thermal conductivity. An example of thermal conductivity is the heat sink. Heat sinks are used in many devices. Today, they are commonly used in computers. A heat sink transfers the heat building up in the computer processor, moving it away before it can damage the processor. Computers contain fans, which blow air across their heat sinks and expel the heated air out of the computers.

## ACOUSTICAL PRINCIPLES AND THE HUMAN HEARING PROCESS

When any physical object moves back and forth rapidly, this is known as vibration. The movements that occur during vibration disturb the surrounding medium, which may be solid, liquid, or gaseous. The most common sound conducting medium in our environment is gaseous: our atmosphere (i.e. the air). An object's vibratory movements represent a form of energy. As this acoustic energy moves through the air, it takes the form of waves, sound waves specifically. The outer ear receives and amplifies the sound and transmits it to the middle ear, where tiny bones vibrate in response to the sound energy and transmit it to the inner ear. The inner ear converts the acoustic energy into electrical energy. The electrical impulses are then carried by nerves to the brain. Structures in the brain associated with hearing receive these electrical signals and interpret them (i.e. make sense of them) as sounds. The ears' reception of sound waves is auditory sensation, and the brain's interpretation of them is auditory perception.

## SOLAR SYSTEM
### SOLAR SYSTEM'S LOCATION AND COMPONENTS

The universe is composed of an unknown (possibly infinite) number of galaxies or star systems, such as the Spiral Nebula, the Crab Nebula, and the Milky Way. Our sun, Sol, is one of billions of stars in the Milky Way. The solar system's planets are held in position at varying distances (according to their size and mass) from the Sun by its gravitational force. These planets orbit or revolve around the Sun. From the closest to the Sun to the farthest away, the solar system's planets are Mercury, Venus, Earth, Mars, Jupiter, Saturn, Uranus, and Neptune. Pluto was historically included as the ninth planet, but was demoted to a "dwarf planet" by the International Astronomical Union in 2006. Due to angular momentum, planets rotate on their axes, which are imaginary central lines between their north and south poles. One complete Earth rotation equals what we perceive as one 24-hour day. As the Earth turns, different portions face the Sun. These receive daylight, while the portions turned away from the Sun are in darkness. One complete revolution of the Earth around the Sun represents one calendar year.

### PLUTO

Since more powerful observatories have enabled greater detection and measurement of celestial objects, the International Astronomical Union has defined three criteria for defining a planet. First, it must orbit the Sun. Pluto meets this criterion. Second, it must have enough gravitational force to shape itself into a sphere. Pluto also meets this criterion. Third, a planet must have "cleared the neighborhood" in its orbit. This expression refers to the fact that as planets form, they become the strongest gravitational bodies within their orbits. Therefore, when close to smaller bodies, planets either consume these smaller bodies or repel them because of their greater gravity, clearing their orbital area/"neighborhood." To do this, a planet's mass must sufficiently exceed the mass of other bodies in its orbit. Pluto does not meet this criterion, having only 0.07 times the mass of other objects within its orbit. Thus, astronomers reclassified Pluto as a "dwarf planet" in 2006 based on its lesser mass and the many other objects in its orbit with comparable masses and sizes.

### EARTH

Earth is roughly spherical in shape. Its North and South Poles at the top and bottom are farthest away from and least exposed to the Sun, so they are always coldest. This accounts for the existence of the polar ice caps. The Equator, an imaginary line running around Earth at its middle exactly halfway between the North and South Poles, is at 0° latitude. Sunrises and sunsets at the Equator are the world's fastest. Days and nights are of virtually equal length at the Equator, and there is less seasonal variation than in other parts of the world. The equatorial climate is a tropical rainforest. Locations close to the North Pole, like Norway, are at such high latitudes that their nights are not dark in summertime, hence the expression "Land of the Midnight Sun." They also have very little light in wintertime. As Earth revolves around the Sun over the course of a year, the distance and angle of various locations relative to the Sun change, so different areas receive varying amounts of heat and light. This is what accounts for the changing seasons.

## ROCKS FOUND ON THE EARTH'S SURFACE
### SEDIMENTARY ROCKS

Earth's rock types are sedimentary, igneous, and metamorphic. These categories are based on the respective processes that form each type of rock. Igneous rocks are formed from volcanoes. Metamorphic rocks are formed when igneous and sedimentary rocks deep inside the Earth's crust are subjected to intense heat and/or pressure. Sedimentary rocks are formed on Earth's surface, and characteristically accumulate in layers. Erosion and other natural processes deposit these layers. Some sedimentary rocks are held together by electrical attraction. Others are cemented

49

together by chemicals and minerals that existed during their formation. Still others are not held together at all, but are loose and crumbly. There are three subcategories of sedimentary rock. Clastic sedimentary rocks are made of little rock bits—clasts—that are compacted and cemented together. Chemical sedimentary rocks are frequently formed through repeated flooding and subsequent evaporation. The evaporation of water leaves a layer of minerals that were dissolved in the water. Limestone and deposits of salt and gypsum are examples. Organic sedimentary rocks are formed from organic matter, such as the calcium left behind from animal bones and shells.

## METAMORPHIC ROCKS

Sedimentary rocks are formed on the Earth's surface by layers of eroded material from mountains that were deposited by water, minerals like lime, salt and gypsum deposited by evaporated floodwater, and organic material like calcium from animal bones and shells. Igneous rocks are formed from liquid volcanic rock—either magma underground or lava on the surface—that cools and hardens. Metamorphic rocks are formed from sedimentary and igneous rocks. This happens when sedimentary and/or igneous rocks are deep inside the Earth's crust, where they are subjected to great pressure or heat. The process of metamorphism does not melt these rocks into liquid, which would happen inside a volcano. Rather, the pressure and/or heat change the rocks' molecular structure. Metamorphic rocks are thus more compact and denser than the sedimentary or igneous rocks from which they were formed. They also contain new minerals produced either by the reconfiguration of existing minerals' structures or by chemical reactions with liquids infiltrating the rock. Two examples of metamorphic rocks are marble and gneiss.

## IGNEOUS ROCKS

Igneous or volcanic rocks are formed from the magma emitted when a volcano erupts. Magma under the Earth's surface is subject to heat and pressure, keeping it in liquid form. During a volcanic eruption, some magma reaches the surface, emerging as lava. Lava cools rapidly in the outside air, becoming a solid with small crystals. Some magma does not reach Earth's surface, but is trapped underground within pockets in other rocks. Magma cools more slowly underground than lava does on the surface. This slower cooling forms rocks with larger crystals and coarser grains. The chemical composition and individual cooling temperatures of magma produce different kinds of igneous rocks. Lava that cools rapidly on the Earth's surface can become obsidian, a smooth, shiny black glass without crystals. It can also become another type of extrusive rock, such as andesite, basalt, pumice, rhyolite, scoria, or tuff (formed from volcanic ash and cinders). Magma that cools slowly in underground pockets can become granite, which has a coarse texture and large, visible mineral grains. It can also become another type of intrusive rock, such as diorite, gabbro, pegmatite, or peridotite.

## EROSION

Erosion is a natural process whereby Earth's landforms are broken down through weathering. Rain, wind, etc. wear away solid matter. Over time, rain reduces mountains to hills. Rocks break off from mountains, and in turn disintegrate into sand. Weathering and the resulting erosion always occur in downhill directions. Rain washes rocks off mountains and down streams. Rains, rivers, and streams wash soils away, and ocean waves break down adjacent cliffs. Rocks, dirt, and sand change their form and location through erosion. They do not simply vanish. These transformations and movements are called mass wasting, which occurs chemically (as when rock is dissolved by chemicals in water) or mechanically (as when rock is broken into pieces). Because materials travel as a result of mass wasting, erosion can both break down some areas and build up others. For example, a river runs through and erodes a mountain, carrying the resulting sediment downstream. This sediment gradually builds up, creating wetlands at the river's mouth. A good example of this

50

process is Louisiana's swamps, which were created by sediment transported by the Mississippi River.

## WEATHER, CLIMATE, AND METEOROLOGY

**Meteorology** is the study of the atmosphere, particularly as it pertains to forecasting the weather and understanding its processes. **Weather** is the condition of the atmosphere at any given moment. Most weather occurs in the troposphere and includes changing events such as clouds, storms, and temperature, as well as more extreme events such as tornadoes, hurricanes, and blizzards. **Climate** refers to the average weather for a particular area over time, typically at least 30 years. Latitude is an indicator of climate. Changes in climate occur over long time periods.

> **Review Video: Climates**
> Visit mometrix.com/academy and enter code: 991320

## WINDS AND GLOBAL WIND BELTS

**Winds** are the result of air moving by convection. Masses of warm air rise, and cold air sweeps into their place. The warm air also moves, cools, and sinks. The term "prevailing wind" refers to the wind that usually blows in an area in a single direction. *Dominant winds* are the winds with the highest speeds. Belts or bands that run latitudinally and blow in a specific direction are associated with *convection cells. Hadley cells* are formed directly north and south of the equator. The *Farrell cells* occur at about 30° to 60°. The jet stream runs between the Farrell cells and the polar cells. At the higher and lower latitudes, the direction is easterly. At mid latitudes, the direction is westerly. From the North Pole to the south, the surface winds are Polar High Easterlies, Subpolar Low Westerlies, Subtropical High or Horse Latitudes, North-East Trade winds, Equatorial Low or Doldrums, South-East Trades, Subtropical High or Horse Latitudes, Subpolar Low Easterlies, and Polar High.

## RELATIVE HUMIDITY, ABSOLUTE HUMIDITY, AND DEW POINT TEMPERATURE

**Humidity** refers to water vapor contained in the air. The amount of moisture contained in air depends upon its temperature. The higher the air temperature, the more moisture it can hold. These higher levels of moisture are associated with higher humidity. **Absolute humidity** refers to the total amount of moisture air is capable of holding at a certain temperature. **Relative humidity** is the ratio of water vapor in the air compared to the amount the air is capable of holding at its current temperature. As temperature decreases, absolute humidity stays the same and relative humidity increases. A hygrometer is a device used to measure humidity. The **dew point** is the temperature at which water vapor condenses into water at a particular humidity.

## PRECIPITATION

After clouds reach the dew point, **precipitation** occurs. Precipitation can take the form of a liquid or a solid. It is known by many names, including rain, snow, ice, dew, and frost. **Liquid** forms of precipitation include rain and drizzle. Rain or drizzle that freezes on contact is known as freezing rain or freezing drizzle. **Solid or frozen** forms of precipitation include snow, ice needles or diamond dust, sleet or ice pellets, hail, and graupel or snow pellets. Virga is a form of precipitation that evaporates before reaching the ground. It usually looks like sheets or shafts falling from a cloud. The amount of rainfall is measured with a rain gauge. Intensity can be measured according to how fast precipitation is falling or by how severely it limits visibility. Precipitation plays a major role in the water cycle since it is responsible for depositing much of the Earth's fresh water.

# CLOUDS

**Clouds** form when air cools and warm air is forced to give up some of its water vapor because it can no longer hold it. This vapor condenses and forms tiny droplets of water or ice crystals called clouds. Particles, or aerosols, are needed for water vapor to form water droplets. These are called **condensation nuclei**. Clouds are created by surface heating, mountains and terrain, rising air masses, and weather fronts. Clouds precipitate, returning the water they contain to Earth. Clouds can also create atmospheric optics. They can scatter light, creating colorful phenomena such as rainbows, colorful sunsets, and the green flash phenomenon.

# LIVING ORGANISMS

All living organisms have fundamental needs that must be met. For example, plants that grow on land need light, air, water, and nutrients in amounts that vary according to the individual plant. Undersea plants may need less/no light. They need gases present in the water, but not in the air above the water. Like land plants, they require nutrients. Like plants, animals (including humans) need air, water, and nutrients. They do not depend on light for photosynthesis like most plants, but some animals require more light than others, while others need less than others or none at all. Organisms cannot survive in environments that do not meet their basic needs. However, many organisms have evolved to adapt to various environments. For example, cacti are desert plants that thrive with only tiny amounts of water, and camels are desert animals that can also go for long periods of time with little water. Penguins and polar bears have adapted to very cold climates. Internal cues (e.g., hunger) and external cues (e.g., environmental change) motivate and shape the behaviors of individual organisms.

# TYPES OF ANIMAL LIFE CYCLES

Most animals, including mammals, birds, fish, reptiles, and spiders, have simple life cycles. They are born live or hatch from eggs, and then grow to adulthood. Animals with simple life cycles include humans. Amphibians like frogs and newts have an additional stage involving a metamorphosis, or transformation. After birth, they breathe through gills and live underwater during youth (e.g., tadpoles). By adulthood, they breathe through lungs and move to land. Butterflies are examples of animals (insects) that undergo complete metamorphosis, meaning they change their overall form. After hatching from an embryo/egg, the juvenile form, or larva, resembles a worm and completes the majority of feeding required. In the next stage, the pupa does not feed, and is typically camouflaged in what is called an inactive stage. Mosquito pupae are called tumblers. The butterfly pupa is called a chrysalis, and is protected by a cocoon. In the final stage, the adult (imago) grows wings (typically) and breeds. Some insects like dragonflies, cockroaches, and grasshoppers undergo an incomplete metamorphosis. There are egg, larva, and adult stages, but no pupa stage.

# ECOLOGY

Ecology is defined as the study of interactions between organisms and their environments. Abiotic factors are the parts of any ecosystem that are not alive, but which affect that ecosystem's living members. Abiotic factors also determine the locations of particular ecosystems that have certain characteristics. Abiotic factors include the sunlight; the atmosphere, including oxygen, hydrogen, and nitrogen; the water; the soil; the temperatures within a system; and the nutrient cycles of chemical elements and compounds that pass among living organisms and their physical environments. Biotic factors are the living organisms within any ecosystem, which include not only humans and animals, but also plants, microorganisms, etc. The definition of biotic factors also includes the interactions that occur between and among various organisms within an ecosystem. Sunlight determines plant growth and, hence, biome locations. Sunlight, in turn, is affected by water

52

depth. Ocean depths where sunlight penetrates, called photic zones, are where the majority of the photosynthesis on Earth occurs.

## ORGANISM REPRODUCTION

A few examples of the many ways in which organisms reproduce include binary fission, whereby the cells of prokaryotic bacteria reproduce; budding, which is how yeast cells reproduce; and asexual reproduction. The latter occurs in plants when they are grafted, when cuttings are taken from them and then rooted, or when they put out runners. Plants also reproduce sexually, as do humans and most other animals. Animals, including humans, produce gametes (i.e. sperm or eggs) in their gonads through the process of meiosis. Gametes are haploid, containing half the number of chromosomes found in the body's cells. During fertilization, the gametes combine to form a zygote, which is diploid. It has the full number of chromosomes (half from each gamete), which are arranged in a genetically unique combination. Zygotes undergo mitosis, reproducing their gene combination with identical DNA sequences in all new cells, which then migrate and differentiate into organizations of specialized organs and tissues. These specialized organs in biologically mature organisms, alerted by signals such as hormonal cues, undergo meiosis to create new haploid gametes, beginning the cycle again.

## PLANT REPRODUCTION

Most plants can reproduce asexually. For example, cuttings can be rooted in water and planted. Some plants put out runners that root new growths. Many plants can be grafted to produce new ones. Plants also reproduce sexually. Plants' sexual life cycles are more complex than animals', since plants alternate between haploid form (i.e. having a single set of chromosomes) and diploid form (i.e. having two sets of chromosome) during their life cycles. Plants produce haploid cells called gametes* (equivalent to sperm and egg in animals) that combine during fertilization, producing zygotes (diploid cells with chromosomes from both gametes). Cells reproduce exact copies through mitosis (asexual reproduction), becoming differentiated/specialized to form organs. Mature diploid plants called sporophytes—the plant form we usually see—produce spores. In sporophytes' specialized organs, cells undergo meiosis. This is part of the process of sexual reproduction, during which cells with half the normal number of chromosomes are produced before fertilization occurs. The spores produced by the sporophyte generation undergo mitosis, growing into a haploid plant of the gametophyte generation that produces gametes*. The cycle then repeats.

## ECOLOGICAL RELATIONSHIPS

Organisms interact, both with other organisms and their environments. Relationships wherein two differing organisms regularly interact so that one or both of them benefit are known as ecological relationships. In mutualistic relationships, both organisms benefit. For example, bacteria live in termites' digestive systems. Termites eat wood. However, they cannot digest the cellulose (the main part of plant cell walls) in wood. The bacteria in termites' guts break down the cellulose for them, releasing the wood's nutrients. Reciprocally, the termites as hosts give the bacteria a home and food. In commensalistic relationships, one organism benefits and the other one is unaffected. One example is barnacles attaching to whales. Barnacles, which are filter feeders, benefit from the whales' swimming, which creates currents in the water that bring the barnacles food. The whales are not disturbed by the barnacles. In parasitic relationships, the parasite benefits, but the host suffers. For example, tapeworms inside animals' digestive tracts get nutrients. The hosts lose the nutrients stolen by the worms, and can sustain tissue damage because of the presence of the tapeworms.

# Health and Physical Education

## Health and Physical Education Foundations

### HUMAN HEALTH AND WELLNESS AND DISEASE PREVENTION

Health and disease prevention begin before birth. Expecting mothers need to be/become informed about good nutrition for all humans and the supplemental nutrition required for prenatal support of developing embryos and fetuses. Mothers also need to get sufficient but not overly strenuous exercise; avoid undue stress; have/learn effective coping skills to deal with unavoidable life stressors; and avoid exposure to environmental toxins, such as radiation, pollution, and chemicals. They should avoid alcohol, tobacco, and exposure to secondhand smoke, as well as most drugs—street, over-the-counter, herbal, and prescription—unless they are prescribed by obstetricians/other physicians who are aware of the pregnancy. Babies initially need their mother's colostrum to provide immunity, and subsequently require breast milk or approved infant formula. Babies must also be held, cuddled, and given attention and affection to ensure survival, growth, and health. Young children need smaller amounts of food than adults that is equally as nutritious; sufficient exercise; adequate sleep; and cognitive, emotional, and social stimulation and interaction. Appropriate nutrition and exercise, avoidance of alcohol/tobacco/other drugs, and positive relationships and interactions are essential for wellness and disease prevention at all ages.

### 2009 AMERICAN RECOVERY AND REINVESTMENT ACT

The 2009 American Recovery and Reinvestment Act has allotted $650 million for preventing chronic disease. To apply these funds, the U.S. Department of Health and Human Services (HHS) has designed a comprehensive initiative entitled Communities Putting Prevention to Work. This initiative aims to create sustainable positive health changes in American communities, prevent or delay chronic disease, reduce disease risk factors, and promote child and adult wellness. Obesity and tobacco use, considered the foremost preventable sources of disability and death, are targeted by this initiative's evidence-based research programs and strategies, which are intended to reinforce state abilities and mobilize community resources. The initiative's central, $373-million community program includes support from the Centers for Disease Control and Prevention in selected communities for attaining the prevention outcomes of increasing physical activity levels, improving nutrition, reducing the incidence of obesity and higher than optimal body weights, decreasing tobacco use, and decreasing secondhand smoke exposure. Through this initiative, HHS hopes to produce effective models that can be reproduced in states and communities nationwide.

### ENVIRONMENTAL HEALTH RISKS

Children's body systems, unlike those of mature adults, are still developing. They eat, drink, and breathe more in proportion to their body sizes than adults do. Typical child behaviors expose children to more potentially toxic chemicals and organisms. Therefore, children can be more vulnerable to environmental health risks. To protect children, adults can prohibit smoking in homes and cars; keep homes free of dust, mold, pet dander, and pests that can trigger allergies; avoid outdoor activities on high-pollution/"ozone alert" days; and carpool and/or use public transportation. Adults can prevent lead poisoning by only giving children cold water to drink and using cold water to prepare infant formula and cook food; washing bottles, pacifiers, and toys frequently; and protecting children from lead-based paints in older buildings. Adults must ensure children do not have access to toxic chemicals. Maintaining furnaces, chimneys, and appliances; using outdoor gas appliances and tools properly; refraining from using gas appliances and tools indoors; and installing approved CO alarms can all help prevent carbon monoxide poisoning.

54

Choosing fish carefully can help prevent mercury toxicity. Keeping infants out of direct sunlight, using sun-protective clothing, and applying sunscreen on young children are also important.

## FEDERAL EXECUTIVE ORDER 13045: PROTECTION OF CHILDREN FROM ENVIRONMENTAL HEALTH RISKS AND SAFETY RISKS (1997)

Passed by President Clinton, Executive Order 13045 declares a policy for identifying and assessing environmental health and safety risks that affect children disproportionately, and for addressing these risks through the policies, standards, programs, and activities of every independent federal regulatory agency. This order defines environmental health and safety risks as those that can be attributed to substances children ingest or contact (e.g., air they breathe; food they eat; water they drink, bathe in, and swim in; soil they live upon; and products they are exposed to or use). The order established a task force reporting to the president and consulting with the Domestic Policy Council, the National Science and Technology Council, the Council on Environmental Quality, and the Office of Management and Budget. The task force is co-chaired by the HHS secretary and the EPA administrator. The task force oversees a coordinated, integrated federal research agenda and reports relevant research/data biennially; issues principle, policy, and priority statements; recommends appropriate federal/state/local/tribal government, nonprofit, and private sector partnerships; makes public outreach/communication proposals; identifies related high-priority initiatives; and evaluates new legislation to determine whether it will meet the goals of Executive Order 13045.

## CIRCULATORY SYSTEM

The circulatory system continuously supplies blood containing oxygen and nutrients to all body tissue cells, exchanges oxygenated blood for the waste products produced during the metabolism process, and transports waste for elimination. Central to the vascular (vessel) system is the heart, which is located in the mediastinum within the thoracic cavity. The heart is encased and protected by the pericardium, a double-walled, tough fibrous sac. The heart has four chambers: two atria and two ventricles. A system of valves regulates opening/closing among the chambers, the aorta, the pulmonary artery, and the great vessels. The aorta, originating at the heart, is the body's largest artery. The pulmonary artery branches to the left and to the right, and transports venous blood from the heart's lower right chamber to the lung for oxygenation. The pulmonary veins return oxygenated blood from the lung to the left atrium of the heart. The superior and inferior venae cavae are vessels that empty into the heart's right atrium.

## INTEGUMENTARY AND MUSCULOSKELETAL SYSTEMS

In the human body, the integumentary system consists of skin, hair, nails, and oil and sweat glands. The skin has three layers: the epidermis, the dermis, and subcutaneous tissues. Skin protects tissues underneath it from bacterial infections, blocks most chemicals from entering, prevents fluid loss, and reduces the probability of mechanical injury to underlying body structures. Skin regulates body temperature and synthesizes needed chemicals. It is also a sense organ, as it has sensory receptors for touch, pressure, heat/cold, and pain. It also contains motor fibers that enable necessary reactions to these sensations and stimuli. The musculoskeletal system includes bones, joints, and connective tissues: tendons, ligaments, and cartilage. It is responsible for our body shape, and provides stability and support. It also protects our internal organs and enables locomotion. Bones store calcium and other minerals, and bone marrow produces required blood cells. Muscle fibers contract to enable movement. Depending on their innervation, muscles can have voluntary or involuntary (like the heart) movements. Muscles need blood supply and oxygen to work. Thus, the musculoskeletal system depends on other systems, including the circulatory, nervous, and respiratory systems.

> **Review Video: Integumentary System**
> Visit mometrix.com/academy and enter code: 655980
>
> **Review Video: Skeletal System**
> Visit mometrix.com/academy and enter code: 256447

## LYMPHATIC SYSTEM

The lymphatic system includes lymph (a fluid), collection ducts, and tissues. Lymphatic tissues comprise the lymph nodes, the thymus gland, the tonsils, and the Peyer's patches of the intestinal tract. Lymphoid components are also present in the lungs, the mucosa in the stomach and the appendix, and the bone marrow. Microscopic capillaries merge to form lymph-collecting ducts. These ducts drain to specific centers of lymphatic tissue. The lymph system's functioning is supported by the spleen and thymus glands. While not all characteristics and functions of the lymphatic system are established, known functions include: return transportation of lymph, protein, and microorganisms to the cardiovascular system; production of lymphocytes by the lymph nodes; filtering of the blood by the lymph nodes; production of antibodies to enable immune response against infection; absorption of fats and fat soluble substances from the intestine; formation of blood cells in response to some illnesses/conditions; and phagocytosis (i.e. the surrounding/swallowing/"eating" of infectious particles by cells lining the sinuses of the lymph nodes, spleen, and liver). The lymph system defends the body against infection and supports the veins by helping to return fluids to the bloodstream.

## RESPIRATORY SYSTEM

The respiratory system provides oxygen to the body and removes carbon dioxide, the waste product of respiration (breathing). In doing so, the respiratory system and many other body systems work together through complex interactions. Twelve thoracic vertebrae, twelve pairs of ribs, the sternum, the diaphragm, and the intercostal muscles comprise the thoracic cage containing the lungs. As one breathes in and out, the thoracic cage is always moving. The diaphragm, a muscular wall dividing the chest cavity and abdominal cavity, functions as a bellows for breathing. (It also plays a role in expelling feces and delivering babies.) There are air pathways between the nose/mouth, pharynx, trachea, bronchi, bronchioles, and lungs. Alveoli, tiny air sacs in the lungs, exchange oxygen and carbon dioxide. During inspiration/inhalation, the ribs and sternum rise, the diaphragm contracts and lowers, the intercostal muscles contract, air pressure in the lungs decreases, and air enters the lungs. During exhalation, the intercostal muscles and diaphragm relax, the ribs and sternum return to a resting position, air pressure in the lungs increases, and air exits the lungs.

> **Review Video: Respiratory System**
> Visit mometrix.com/academy and enter code: 783075

## THE BRAIN

The brain is divided into five major parts: the cerebrum, the midbrain, the cerebellum, the pons, and the medulla oblongata. The cranial nerves are: I – olfactory, which controls the sense of smell; II – optic, which controls vision; III – oculomotor, which controls the movements of the eye muscles, the movements of the upper eyelids, and the pupillary reflexes (expanding and contracting to admit more/less light); IV – trochlear, which controls the movements of the superior oblique eye muscles; V – trigeminal, which controls facial sensation, the eye's corneal reflex, and chewing; VI – abducens, which controls the movements of the lateral rectus eye muscle; VII – facial, which controls movement of the facial muscles and the taste sensation in the front two-thirds of the tongue; VIII – vestibulocochlear, which controls equilibrium (balance) via the vestibular system in the inner ear, and hearing (the cochlea is in the inner ear); IX – glossopharyngeal, which controls the taste sensation in the rear one-third of the tongue; X – vagus, which controls pharyngeal contraction (gag reflex), vocal cord movements, and soft palate movements; XI – spinal accessory, which controls movement of the sternocleidomastoid and trapezius muscles; and XII – hypoglossal, which controls tongue movements.

> **Review Video: Brain Anatomy**
> Visit mometrix.com/academy and enter code: 222476

## CENTRAL NERVOUS SYSTEM

Some main functions of the central nervous system (i.e. the brain and spinal cord) include controlling consciousness and all mental processes, regulating the functions and movements of the body, and sending and receiving nerve impulses to and from all parts of the body. For example, when we touch something hot, sensory nerve endings in our fingers send impulses to the brain, which interprets them as heat and sends a signal along motor nerves to pull our fingers away. The autonomic nervous system is automatic and involuntary. For example, it makes our heart beat. We cannot voluntarily start/stop our heartbeat. The voluntary nervous system is under our conscious control. For example, our brains use it to send impulses to our skeletal muscles when we want to sit/stand/walk, etc., which contract in response. The autonomic nervous system is divided into parasympathetic and sympathetic components. The parasympathetic portion stimulates muscular activity in the organs and gland secretion. The sympathetic portion stimulates heartbeat, vasoconstriction, and sweating. These two portions of the autonomic nervous system oppose/balance each other to regulate system

## DIGESTIVE SYSTEM

The chief functions of the digestive system are to provide nutrition to the body's cells and eliminate waste products left after nourishment is extracted from foods. The process consists of three phases: ingestion (i.e. taking in foods and liquids), digestion (i.e. converting ingested nutrients through physical and chemical means into forms that the cells of the body tissues can absorb and distribute), and elimination (i.e. removing the byproducts of digestion—also known as waste—that cannot be utilized). Other body systems work with the digestive system to process nutrients. For example, the nervous system plays a role in appetite, which is a signal for us to eat. The central nervous system also stimulates the release and flow of digestive juices. The endocrine system supplies chemicals (e.g., juices from the pancreas) that aid in digestion. The circulatory system delivers digested and absorbed nutrients to the tissue cells, and also picks up waste products produced as a result of the metabolism process.

During chewing, our teeth and tongue physically break down food. Glands secrete saliva to provide lubrication during chewing and swallowing, and provide digestive enzymes to begin the process of chemically breaking down the foods we eat. The pharynx delivers food to the esophagus, where muscular contractions (peristalsis) move food downward. The epiglottis closes the trachea (windpipe) during swallowing to prevent food from being aspirated into the lungs. Glands in the stomach lining secrete gastric fluid comprised of hydrochloric acid and other chemicals, which dissolve food into semiliquid chyme. Chyme gradually passes into the small intestine, where most digestion and absorption occur. The small intestine is made up of the duodenum, the jejunum, and the ileum. The pancreas secretes digestive juices, the gallbladder secretes bile, and the intestinal mucosa secretes other juices into the duodenum to digest chyme. Digested nutrients are absorbed through the intestinal walls into capillaries and lymphatic vessels to be distributed to body cells. The large intestine consists of the cecum, the colon (ascending, transverse, descending, and sigmoid), the rectum, and the anus. The colon completes digestion and absorption, and delivers wastes to the rectum, which eliminates them through the anus.

> **Review Video: Gastrointestinal System**
> Visit mometrix.com/academy and enter code: 378740

## URINARY SYSTEM

The function of the urinary system is to eliminate the liquid wastes produced through nutrient metabolism by excreting them from the body. The urinary system is made up of two kidneys, two ureters, the bladder, and the urethra. Behind the abdominal cavity at the thoraco-lumbar level are the kidneys, a pair of large bean-shaped glands. They continually remove water, salts, toxins, and nitrogenous wastes from the bloodstream, and convert these substances into urine. Urine droplets flow from the kidneys into the ureters. The ureters are long, narrow tubes carrying urine to the bladder, which is a hollow, muscular, elastic organ. When enough urine collects in the bladder, nerves stimulate the body to empty it via urination. In human females, the urethra is about an inch and a half long, and is located in the upper vaginal wall. In males, the urethra is about eight inches long, and extends from the bladder through the prostate gland and the penis. Both urine and sperm pass through the male urethra, while the female urethra and vaginal canal are separate.

> **Review Video: Urinary System**
> Visit mometrix.com/academy and enter code: 601053

## ENDOCRINE SYSTEM

The human endocrine system is one of the most complex body systems. Scientists understand many of its functions, but not all of them. It is a system of ductless, internally secreting glands (some necessary to life) that extract various substances from tissue fluids and the bloodstream to create completely new substances (i.e. hormones). Operating without ducts, endocrine glands secrete hormones directly into the blood and lymph circulatory systems for distribution to the organs. The endocrine system's main glands include the pituitary, thyroid, parathyroid, and adrenal glands; the Islets of Langerhans in the pancreas; and the gonads (male testes and female ovaries). Additionally, the pancreas is both an endocrine and an exocrine gland. Its endocrine (internal secretion) function is to secrete insulin to regulate sugar metabolism; its exocrine (external secretion) function is to secrete pancreatic juice into the duodenum to aid in digestion. If the pancreas produces insufficient insulin, type 1 diabetes results. If the body responds insufficiently to insulin, type 2 diabetes results.

> **Review Video: Endocrine System**
> Visit mometrix.com/academy and enter code: 678939

### PITUITARY, THYROID, AND PARATHYROID GLANDS

The pituitary and thyroid glands are both components of the endocrine system. The pituitary gland functions directly by regulating physical growth, development, and sexual maturation in children and adolescents; regulating the retention and excretion of fluid; regulating the balance of electrolytes (sodium, potassium, and chloride) in blood and tissues; and regulating new mothers' lactation (milk production). The pituitary is termed the hypophyseal /"master gland" because it also regulates all other glands in the endocrine system. Therefore, it is involved in regulating food assimilation and metabolism through hydrating the thyroid gland; regulating body composition, adaptation, and resistance to stress through acting on the adrenal and parathyroid glands; regulating breathing, circulation, digestion, urine excretion, and muscular action through the

58

collective activity of multiple hormones; and regulating sexual development, activity, and reproduction through acting on the gonads. The thyroid gland manufactures and secretes hormones that regulate child growth and development, as well as certain metabolic processes and their rates. It also stores iodine. The parathyroid glands secrete hormones that regulate blood calcium levels, phosphorus metabolism, and muscle and nervous system excitation.

## REPRODUCTIVE SYSTEM

### MALE

The scrotum and the penis are the external reproductive organs of the human male. The internal organs of the male reproductive system include two testes, two epididymides, two seminal ducts, two seminal vesicles, two ejaculatory ducts, two spermatic cords, the urethra, the prostate gland, and several other glands. The testes, which are glandular organs, hang on either side of the scrotum from spermatic cords. These cords contain the vas deferens, blood vessels, and supportive tissues. Male sperm cells and hormones are produced by the testes. Each testis has an epididymis connecting it to the vas deferens, an excretory seminal duct. The vas deferens travel upward inside the spermatic cords to the prostate gland, which is in front of the neck of the urinary bladder. There, the vas deferens join with the pouch-like glands called seminal vesicles to form ejaculatory ducts. The prostate gland and seminal vesicles secrete substances into the semen that promote sperm motility. The ejaculatory ducts release semen into the urethra, and from here the semen is ejected through the penis during sexual intercourse.

### FEMALE

The external female reproductive organs include the mons pubis, the labia majora, the labia minora, the clitoris, the vestibule, the hymen, the Bartholin's glands, and several other glands. The breasts/mammary glands can also be considered parts of the reproductive system, as they produce milk for infants following reproduction. Internal organs include the vagina, the two fallopian tubes, the uterus, and the two ovaries. Hormones stimulate either ovary to produce an ovum/egg roughly once a month. A follicle containing an egg cell forms. When the egg matures, the follicle ruptures, releasing the egg. This is known as ovulation. The ovum passes into a fallopian tube and travels toward the uterus. Hormones have meanwhile also stimulated the endometrium (uterine lining) to thicken and increase its blood supply. When the egg reaches the womb, it is implanted in the endometrium if it was fertilized in the fallopian tube by a male sperm. This is known as conception. If the egg was not fertilized, hormone signals subside, causing the endometrium to detach from the uterine wall. The sloughed off endometrial tissue, the resulting blood, and the unfertilized egg exit the body. This process is known as menstruation.

## INFLUENCE OF PHYSICAL, EMOTIONAL, AND SOCIAL FACTORS ON PERSONAL PHYSICAL HEALTH

The parts of the body, including the brain, are connected, related, interactive, and interdependent. As humans also interact and are interdependent with their environment, both internal and external factors influence their health. For example, physical factors like exposure to air pollution or radiation can cause illnesses like asthma, other lung diseases, and various cancers. Too much or too little nutrition can cause obesity and diabetes* or malnutrition. Too much or too little exercise can cause exhaustion and injuries or weakness, diabetes*, and cardiovascular and pulmonary problems. Not exercising enough may also be a factor in being overweight or obese. *Diabetes itself causes many related health problems, including blindness, circulatory deficiencies, amputation, and cardiovascular disease. Water and/or sleep deprivation ultimately cause death. Emotional factors like depression, anxiety, and irritability can cause a host of health problems, including insomnia, overeating, anorexia, high blood pressure, and heart disease. Social factors include family influences. According to the family systems theory, dysfunctional family dynamics can cause a child

59

to develop a physical illness. Whether the source is family, society outside the home, or both, stress is a social influence with multiple negative health impacts.

## EFFECT OF NUTRITION ON DEVELOPMENT

Children must consume a full range of nutrients for their brains to work normally. They need protein for its amino acids, which enable the brain's neurotransmitters (chemical messengers) to fire and communicate with each other. They need fruit and vegetable sugars and other complex carbohydrates to supply fuel to power the brain's functioning. Children's nutrition begins before birth. Pregnant women who do not eat adequate nutrients, vitamins, and minerals have higher risks of delivering infants with low birth weights. Research has found that babies with low birth weights are more likely to experience hearing and vision problems, and to need special education services in school at some point. Children in school who consume insufficient amounts of protein have been found to score lower on achievement tests than their peers who are getting enough protein. Children with iron deficiencies display fatigue and ADHD-like symptoms, including impaired concentration, shortened attention spans, and irritability. Children who miss breakfast consistently perform slower on problem solving tests than those who do not. Their responses are also less accurate. Children who regularly miss meals have compromised immunity against illnesses and infections, and they miss more school.

## MOTOR SKILLS

Motor skills are the large and small movements of the body. These movements include such things as pushing, pulling, lifting, and carrying larger objects using the legs, arms, and back; and picking up, grasping, and manipulating smaller objects using the hands and fingers. The former are gross motor skills, and the latter are fine motor skills. To develop these, children must make effective use of their mind-body connection (i.e. getting the muscles and bones to perform the movements the mind intends). They must also have developed spatial awareness (i.e. an accurate sense of the relationship between their bodies and the surrounding space and other bodies/objects). Teaching children to move large and small muscles in time to rhythmic songs helps develop motor skills. Teaching directions like up, down, clockwise, counterclockwise, etc. helps with motor planning development. When children find motor skills challenging to master, educators must provide them with frequent instruction, adequate re-teaching, and ample modeling that allows them to observe and imitate problematic movements.

## FINE MOTOR MOVEMENTS

Fine motor movements use small muscles in the eyes, lips, tongue, wrists, fingers, and toes. Fine/small motor movements work together with gross/large muscle movements to develop movement skills and patterns. Fine motor skills are often used for purposes of functional and expressive communication, like using tools, creating artworks, and writing and typing language. Eye-hand coordination, eye-foot coordination, and manual and finger dexterity are required for the fine motor movements used in drawing, writing, and typing. Fine motor practice also develops children's tactile (touch) awareness and spatial awareness. Rolling dough/putty/clay into balls and/or hiding things inside them promote fine motor skills. Tearing and cutting paper along dotted lines and creating patterns teach accurate size and shape perception and formation. Stringing, lacing, and creating structures using plastic building blocks develop hand-eye coordination and skills needed to create color patterns. Flip cards, pegs, and stickers promote object placement skills. Writing skills are developed by writing letters/numbers in shaving cream, sand, pudding, and/or on chalkboards using wet makeup sponges/cotton swabs; using toothbrushes on dry erase boards; and practicing placement on cardboard using rice, beans, wet/dry pasta, glitter, etc.

## GROSS MOTOR SKILLS

The first motor movements of EC are gross motor skills (i.e. large body movements involving the torso, limbs, and feet). Sitting, standing, crawling, walking, running, galloping, jumping, catching, throwing, and kicking use these skills. Activities that help young children develop their gross motor skills include standing on dots/marks on the floor/ground; crawling under and climbing over things, including objects that are part of obstacle courses; and balancing on balance beams. These develop body control, coordination, laterality (using the left/right sides of the body separately), and synchronization of the body's left and right sides. Children develop body control and balance through hopping around objects. They develop coordination and overall gross motor skills through jumping over things like boxes, beanbags, lines/strings; and by kicking balls, balloons, etc. of various sizes. Walking and running around, through, and/or over obstacles like tires, hoops, etc. and/or participating in relays develop gross motor skills. Organized games involving skipping around things to music with various rhythms, and activities requiring twisting, turning, and bending all develop gross motor skills, preparing children for lifelong engagement in sports activities.

## NEWBORN/INFANT MOTOR REFLEXES AND SKILLS

Newborns exhibit the tonic reflex, adopting the "fencing position." In this position, the head is turned to one side, the arm on that side is in front of the eyes, and the other arm is flexed. This normally disappears by the time an infant is around four months old. It may serve as preparation for reaching voluntarily for things/people. The stepping reflex disappears at around two months of age, and prepares babies for walking voluntarily. The palmar grasping reflex on an adult finger disappears by the time an infant is around three to four months old, and prepares babies for grasping voluntarily. When held upright, a baby can typically hold his/her head steady and erect by about six weeks of age on average. About 90 percent of infants will develop this skill between the ages of three weeks and four months. Babies lift up from the prone position using their arms by the time they are about two months old. About 90 percent of infants will develop this skill between the ages of three weeks and four months. Babies can also roll from side to back by the time they are about two months old. About 90 percent of infants will develop this skill between the ages of three weeks and five months. An infant can grasp a cube by the age of three months and three weeks on average. About 90 percent of infants will develop this skill between the ages of two and seven months.

## INFANT MOTOR SKILLS MILESTONES

By four and a half months on average, babies can roll from back to side. The range within which 90 percent of infants will be able to do this is two to seven months. Most babies can sit unsupported by seven months on average. The range within which 90 percent of infants will be able to do this is five to nine months. Most infants also crawl by seven months on average. The range within which 90 percent of infants will be able to do this is five to eleven months. Babies pull themselves up to a standing position by around eight months on average. The range within which 90 percent of infants will be able to do this is five to twelve months. Babies play "patty-cake" by nine months, three weeks on average. The range within which 90 percent of infants will be able to do this is seven to fifteen months. Babies/toddlers can stand alone by 11 months on average. The range within which 90 percent of infants will be able to do this is 9 to 16 months. Toddlers can walk unassisted by the age of 11 months, 3 weeks on average. The range within which 90 percent of infants will be able to do this is 9 to 17 months. Children can stack two cubes by the age of 13 months, 3 weeks on average. The range within which 90 percent of infants will be able to do this is 10 to 19 months. They scribble energetically by the age of 14 months on average. The range within which 90 percent of infants will be able to do this is 10 to 21 months. They can climb stairs with assistance by the age

**61**

of 16 months on average. The range within which 90 percent of infants will be able to do this is 12 to 23 months. Normally developing children can typically can jump in place by the age of 23 months, 2 weeks on average. The range within which 90 percent of infants will be able to do this is 17 to 30 months.

## CEPHALOCAUDAL AND PROXIMODISTAL DEVELOPMENT

Infant and child motor development follows the same developmental sequences as prenatal embryonic and fetal physical development. Cephalocaudal means head to tail. Just as the body develops from the head down before birth, babies and young children develop motor control of their heads before they develop control of their legs. Proximodistal means near to far (i.e. central to distant). Head, torso, and arm control develop before hand and finger control. Babies learn a lot about how things look, sound, and feel once they master gross motor skills for reaching and grasping. These then evolve toward fine motor skills. For example, at around three months of age an infant's voluntary reaching gradually becomes more accurate. The infant will not need arm guidance, because he or she has spatial awareness of location and motion. Babies reach less by five months when they can move things within reach. By nine months, babies can redirect reaching to grasp objects moving in different directions. By six to twelve months, development of the pincer grasp enhances babies' capacities for object manipulation.

## MOTOR SKILLS DEVELOPING BETWEEN AGES 2 AND 6

Children develop motor skills most quickly between the ages of two and six years. They demonstrate basic locomotion skills, first walking and then running, skipping, hopping, galloping, and jumping. They also develop ball-handling skills, fine motor eye-hand coordination, and—as an extension of previously developed creeping skills—climbing skills. By two years of age, children develop balance for basic kicking, which evolves into the ability to execute full kicks (including backswings) by six years of age. They try throwing by two to three years of age. They develop related skills—including taking a forward step—by the age of six. They develop the ability to shuffle by three years of age, which develops into the ability to skip by six years of age. By the age of three, children walk automatically. They try running, but they are clumsy and lack adequate control. This ability improves by between four and five years of age. By this time, children are also more skilled at executing starts, stops, and turns. By the age of five or six, children can run like adults. They develop climbing skills (ladders, etc.) between the ages of three and six. The ability to jump longer distances and hopping and galloping skills develop by age six. Children can catch a large ball while holding their arm straight by the age of three. They can catch a ball while holding their elbows out to the front by age four, and they can do this while holding their elbows at their sides by age six.

## HOW COOKING AND SELF-CARE ACTIVITIES HELP DEVELOP FINE MOTOR SKILLS

Young children are often fascinated by adults' cooking activities, want to participate, and offer to help. Involving them is not only beneficial to their self-esteem, but also develops various skills. Measuring amounts of liquids and solids in different forms develops children's math skills. Mixing, stirring, and blending ingredients using different parts of their hands develop children's fine motor skills. Life skills include self-care skills, such as combing one's hair, brushing one's teeth, fastening and unfastening buttons and snaps on clothing, and lacing and unlacing shoes. Life skills also require being able to open and close drawers, doors, and jars; to clean a house; and to wash things. It is necessary to children's normal development that they learn to combine multiple fine motor skills. Children's development of fine motor skills also needs to be integrated with the development of various self-care and other life skills (such as those described above) that are required for normal activities of daily living.

## BENEFITS OF PHYSICAL ACTIVITY

When young children engage in physical activity, they learn new motor skills and reinforce, advance, and refine existing ones. They also learn important early math skills like spatial awareness. Whenever they attempt new activities, they encounter challenges, such as having to develop higher levels of coordination, control, precision, strength, speed, flexibility, and agility. They are also challenged to coordinate their mental and physical processes more closely and in a manner that is more complex. They learn to exert effort, and to persevere in the face of difficulty. When they succeed at meeting these challenges, their self-esteem and self-efficacy (sense of competence to perform tasks) are enhanced. Since motor skills generally develop ahead of language skills, physical activity is a valuable means of direct self-expression. Young children learn many social skills through interacting with peers and adults during physical games, sports activities, etc. In addition to all these benefits, young children normally seek out physical activity, deriving a great deal of fun and enjoyment through moving, playing games/sports, and interacting physically with others.

## NATIONAL PHYSICAL EDUCATION STANDARDS

The National Association for Sport and Physical Education (NASPE) has developed six national physical education standards. These standards state that someone who is physically educated: (1) shows the motor skills and patterns of movement competencies s/he needs to conduct various physical activities; (2) shows comprehension of the basic concepts, main principles, methods, and techniques of movement as they relate to learning and executing physical activities; (3) regularly engages in physical activity; (4) reaches and sustains a level of physical fitness that enhances health; (5) demonstrates behaviors, personally and socially, that reflect self-respect and respect for others within contexts of physical activity; and (6) places value upon the benefits of physical activities and of being fit and active, such as the pleasure; the improvement and maintenance of health; the physical, personal, and social challenges; and the opportunities to interact socially and express oneself.

## PHYSICAL, EMOTIONAL, AND SOCIAL FACTORS

Young children who have already become overweight/obese because of an improper diet and lack of exercise are more likely than children who are within a healthy weight range to find physical activity uncomfortable and avoid it. Even those who enjoy activity are more at risk of injury if they are overweight or lack physical conditioning. Exercise is more challenging for children with illnesses. For example, asthma interferes with breathing. Therefore, asthmatic children must be supervised and monitored when exercising. So must diabetic children, whose blood sugar can fluctuate excessively due to exercising. Their food intake must be monitored and coordinated with exercise. Children with physical disabilities may require adaptive equipment and/or alternative methods of physical instruction and exercising. Emotionally, children experiencing depression are likely to be apathetic and uninterested in movement. Hyperactive children (e.g., those with ADHD) are often overactive physically to the point of exhaustion. Children lacking adequate social skills, friends, and/or peer groups have fewer opportunities and are less likely to engage in physical games and sports with others, so their motor skills and physical fitness may suffer.

## AMOUNTS AND PROPORTIONS OF ENGAGEMENT IN PHYSICAL ACTIVITY

The World Health Organization (WHO) advises that children between the ages of 5 and 17 should engage in a minimum of 1 hour (continuously or incrementally) of moderate to vigorous physical activity per day. According to the World Health Organization, exercising for more than one hour daily (within reason) will confer additional health benefits. The majority of children's physical activity should be aerobic in nature. Aerobic exercise uses large muscle groups, is rhythmic and continuous, and works the heart and lungs so that the pulmonary and cardiovascular systems become more efficient at absorbing and transporting oxygen. Children should take part in exercises and/or activities that strengthen the muscles and bones through weight bearing and other methods at least three times per week. Children's play activities that can fulfill bone-strengthening requirements include running, jumping, turning, and playing various games. Engaging in general play, playing games, playing sports, doing chores, using exercise as a means of transportation (e.g., walking, biking, etc.), participating in planned exercise sessions, and attending physical education classes are all activities available in family, community, and school settings that can allow children to meet physical activity and fitness requirements.

# Creative and Performing Arts

## Fine Arts Foundations and Creativity

### LEARNING OUTCOMES ACHIEVED THROUGH VISUAL ARTS

The arts are just as important to include in curricula as language, math, science, social studies, health, and physical education. Early learning standards in many states now reflect the goal to integrate the arts into the overall curriculum. Teachers need to provide young children with activities that promote development of fine motor skills, exploration of art materials and processes, and symbolic representation of concepts through artworks. EC educators should not merely assign isolated art activities. They can clarify many concepts and improve learning by providing art projects that fit into the overall curriculum and are relevant to individual learning units. Teachers should develop detailed, well-organized step lists for each activity. Clear directions not only maintain classroom order, but also provide children with a structure within which to experiment with art and enhance their sequencing skills. Teachers should use process-oriented activities, both on their own and within lessons that require products. For example, painting pictures of animals combines product (representing an animal) with process (exploring paint use). Teachers should supply and explain rules/steps for process activities that explore the use of art materials and processes.

### PLANNING ART ACTIVITIES OR PROJECTS

EC teachers should first establish the concept they want to teach, the objectives they want to meet through planning and teaching the lesson/activity, and the learning objectives they want the children to meet through participating. Then, a teacher can construct a simple prototype for the project. This enables the teacher to estimate how long it will take the children to complete the activity, and to explore and discover the optimal sequencing of steps for the activity. The teacher should then write down the plan, step-by-step. Steps should include those that need to be completed before the activity. These might include preliminary discussion, book reading/sharing related to the project, viewing related artworks and/or photos, etc. Steps should also include those that need to be completed while setting up the activity, such as dispensing paints, clay, etc.; assembling paintbrushes/other instruments; and passing out paper and other materials. Teachers do not need to be artistically proficient. Young children are not art critics, and teachers can find a great deal of information about art materials and processes by reading books and searching online. Available professional development courses focusing on art can also give teachers more ideas for lesson plans.

### FUNCTIONS OF ART

#### SOCIAL FUNCTIONS

Artworks can be created for physical, social, and personal purposes. When art focuses on the social lives of groups rather than on one individual's experiences or viewpoint, it serves social functions. Art carrying political stances/messages always performs social functions. Dadaist Oppenheim's hair-covered tea set did not perform any physical function, but served social functions by politically protesting World War I and many other social/political issues. During the Great Depression, photographers like Dorothea Lange, Gordon Parks, Walker Evans, and Arthur Rothstein commissioned by the Farm Security Administration produced stark records of people's suffering. These depictions of social conditions also served social functions. Fine artists like Francisco Goya and William Hogarth, as well as cartoonists like Thomas Nast and Charles Bragg, created satirical works of art lampooning various social and political customs and situations. Satire is intended not only to provide comic relief, insight, and perspective, but also to stimulate social change. Therefore, it serves social functions. Another social function is improving community status and pride through art treasures.

## PHYSICAL FUNCTIONS

Ascertaining the function of a work of art requires considering its context. Half of the context involves the artist. Knowing the artist's country, the historical time period during which the artist lived, and the social and political culture of the time informs artwork and our ability to infer what the artist was thinking and intending when he or she was creating it. The other half of the context involves the viewer. Knowing what the artwork means to you in your own place and time informs your perception of and response to it. Taken within context, art serves physical, personal, and social functions. For example, architecture, industrial design, and crafts have physical functions. A raku pottery bowl made in Japan serves a physical function during a tea ceremony. However, a teacup covered with hair (paired with a hair-covered saucer and spoon) by Dada artist Meret Oppenheim (1936) makes an artistic statement, but serves no physical function. When we view a tribal war club in a museum, regardless of the exquisite craftsmanship it may demonstrate, we realize it was made primarily for bludgeoning enemies.

## PERSONAL FUNCTIONS

Works of art can have physical, social, and personal functions. Of these three, the personal functions of art are the most variable. Artists' motivations to create works include the desire to express their feelings and ideas, to obtain gratification through producing art, to communicate messages to viewers, to enable both themselves and their viewers to have an aesthetic experience, and to simply entertain viewers. Some artists also claim that they sometimes create art for no particular reason, and that the art produced has no meaning. Art can perform a personal function of control. For example, some artists use their work to give order to the world's apparent chaos. Others use art to create chaos in an overly orderly, boring environment. Art can be therapeutic for both artists and viewers. Much art has served the personal function of religion. Artworks with biological purposes, like cultural fertility symbols or bodily decorations designed to attract mates for procreation, are also examples of the personal functions of art.

## LEARNING OBJECTIVES

When children participate in teacher-designed art activities, they can fulfill learning objectives such as exploring various art materials and processes; developing awareness of visual art and its basic elements (e.g., line, shape, color, and texture); using art forms to represent feelings, thoughts, and/or stories; developing the skills of color recognition and discrimination; and even building their vocabularies and language skills, depending on the activities. Teachers can integrate such objectives with an overall theme for each art activity/project that they integrate with the current theme for their lesson or curriculum unit. For example, if space travel is the class theme one week, constructing model rocket ships is more appropriate than painting self-portraits. Even open-ended activities to explore art materials and processes can be integrated with thematic units. For example, teachers can apply activities exploring cutting and gluing processes to a theme of one specific color by providing various materials and textures that are all the same color. In this way, teachers can connect a learning concept to experimentation with artistic processes.

## CREATING, PERFORMING, AND RESPONDING

Three processes common to all branches of the arts—visual, musical, dance, dramatic, and performance art—are creating, performing, and responding. The first of these, creating, involves the genesis of the artistic product. There are several steps in creating. (1) Imagining is the step during which the artist develops his/her ideas and considers the concepts and feelings which s/he wants to communicate and express through the work. (2) Planning is the step during which the artist researches, experiments with, and designs the means by which s/he will present her/his ideas and emotions (e.g., the materials that will be used and how they will be manipulated to produce the desired effects). (3) Making, evaluating, and refining is the step during which the artist applies her/his skills and various techniques to create an artistic product that will bring her/his ideas and feelings to life. (4) Presenting is the step during which the artist exhibits visual art in a gallery, private exhibit, or another type of showing. The artist might also perform music, dance, theater, or performance art for an audience so that others can participate in and respond to the artwork.

## PROCESSES INVOLVED IN THE PRODUCTION AND RECEPTION OF WORKS OF ART

In all branches of the arts, artists and their audiences (who may also be participants in the case of performance art) complete three basic artistic processes that are closely related: creation, performance, and response. The performance process includes five steps. (1) Selecting is the step during which the artist makes a choice about what to present. For example, musicians choose pieces to play. Dancers choose choreographic pieces to perform. Visual artists select which of their paintings, drawings, sculptures, mobiles/stabiles etc. to display. Theater producers, directors, and actors choose a play to perform. (2) Analyzing is the step during which the performer researches the background of the chosen work and analyzes its structure to understand it and its import. (3) Interpreting is the step during which the performer develops a personal idea about what the work should express or accomplish. (4) Rehearsing, evaluating, and refining is the step during which the performer applies her/his skills and techniques to develop a personal interpretation that will enable her/his performance to make the work come alive. The artist then evaluates the performance, and makes further refinements to subsequent presentations. (5) Presenting is the final step, during which the artist performs the work for others.

## FUNDAMENTAL ARTISTIC PROCESSES COMMON TO ALL BRANCHES OF THE ARTS

Works of art, whether visual, musical, dramatic, literary, dance, or performance art, all involve three basic and interrelated processes: creation of the work, performance of the work for others, and response of others (e.g., audiences, participants, viewers, or readers). The artistic process of responding to artwork includes four steps. (1) Selection is the step during which the person(s) who will receive the artwork choose what they want to experience (possible choices include attending a gallery exhibit of paintings, drawings, or sculptures; going to see a theatrical play or a movie; attending a dance performance; attending/participating in a performance art show; or reading a book of poetry or prose). (2) Analysis is the step during which the viewers/audience/participants/readers see/hear and understand the components of the work, and mentally bring these components together to perceive the work as a whole. (3) Interpretation is the step during which those experiencing the work and/or its performance construct meaning from what they have witnessed, developing a personal response to the creator(s)' and performer(s)' expressions of concepts and emotions. (4) Evaluation is the final step, during which the respondent(s) assess the quality of the artwork and of its performance.

## FACILITATING STUDENT LEARNING WITH CREATING, PERFORMING, AND RESPONDING

The artistic processes have many steps in common. This interrelatedness among the processes informs students' development of educated responses to artworks. For instance, when students learn the step of evaluating their own artworks, they learn to apply better critical approaches when interpreting the artworks created by others. They also use their experiences to direct their selection of works they want to witness and respond to in the future. When students learn how to evaluate and refine their own work, this facilitates their subsequent evaluation and selection of others' works to watch, to perform themselves, and/or to purchase. Teachers can promote this by encouraging students to transfer their learning from one artistic process to another. For example, teachers can introduce students to others' work while they are creating their own so they can transfer what they learn about the creation process to the responding process. When students are solving specific creative/artistic problems, teachers can expose them to other artists' solutions and encourage students to consider these solutions.

## LINES

In visual media, a line is the path of a moving point; the edge of a flat or two-dimensional shape; or the outline of a solid, three-dimensional object. Lines are longer than they are wide. The term measure refers to the width of a line. Lines can be straight, curved, wavy, angular, or zigzag. Lines can be horizontal (side to side), vertical (up and down), or diagonal (at an angle between vertical and horizontal). Lines can also be implied. In this case, they are not physically present, but the artist's arrangement of other elements suggests lines, which organize the picture and/or guide viewers' eyes. The movement a line follows/appears to show is called direction. Where and how a line is placed in a picture/design is called location. Lines define areas, and imply or create open or closed shapes like circles, rectangles, etc. Line combined with shape creates implied volume in paintings/drawings and actual volume in sculptures. Lines express various qualities by being jagged, loopy, bold, repetitive, etc., and evoke different emotional and mental viewer responses.

## SHAPE, FORM, AND VALUE

Shape refers to two-dimensional areas created by connecting lines to outline the contours of objects depicted in art. Shapes can be positive or negative (i.e. defined not by their own outlines, but by the edges of surrounding shapes). Shapes may be biomorphic (i.e. shapes found in nature) or geometric. Variations in value, texture, or color can make shapes stand out in a piece. Form is the three-dimensional projection of shape. Form has dimension and volume. In paintings and drawings, form appears to have mass, while in sculptures it actually does have mass. The term "form" can also be used to describe an artwork's overall structure. Value refers to the appearance and range of lights and darks seen in a visual work of art. Regardless of color, value varies between black and white, with an indefinite range of various shades of gray between these two absolutes.

## TEXTURE AND SPACE

Texture refers to how rough or smooth a surface appears and/or feels. Everyday materials have texture, as do works of art. An object or a work of art can look and/or feel spongy or glassy, wet or dry, soft or hard, etc. Texture can be real, as with sandpaper and other rough-textured materials used to create works of art. Or, it can be illusory, as when materials appear hard or soft, but are really not. Space is defined as the measurable distance between predetermined points. It can be shallow or limited, with a foreground and a background; or it can be deep or extended, with a middle ground as well as a foreground and a background. Two-dimensional space has height and width; three-dimensional space has height and width, plus volume and time. Like negative shape (shape that is not defined by its own outlines, but by the surrounding shapes and their outlines), negative space appears in art. It is the space around and between the positive objects or shapes depicted. This negative space forms its own shapes around positive subjects.

## RHYTHM

In visual art, rhythm is achieved through repeating visual movement. Visual movement is created by arranging lines, shapes, and/or colors to give the viewer's eye a sense of motion and direction. Just as we hear rhythm in music through aural beats and varying note durations, we see rhythm in paintings through visual movement of lines, angles, shapes, and other elements. Just as Beethoven used repetition of musical phrases and themes to create mood, drama, and movement, artists use movement and repetition to create visual rhythm. For example, in "Nude Descending a Staircase,

68

No. 2" (1912) by Marcel Duchamp, the artist depicts an abstracted human figure, repeating the figure using overlapping placements in a diagonal, downward pattern. The series of repeated shapes and angles gives the impression of viewing action in strobe lighting or via stop action photography. The figures are physically still, but visually convey the effect of moving down a staircase. By directionally repeating the figure, Duchamp shows movement and rhythm within the static medium of a painting.

## COLOR

Color refers to the wavelengths of light reflected by a surface. Some wavelengths are absorbed by paints and other visual art media/materials; we do not see these. Other wavelengths are reflected; these are the ones we see as colors. Primary colors are pure, individual colors that cannot be separated into other colors or produced by mixing colors. The three primary colors are red, blue, and yellow. Secondary colors are combinations of two primary colors (e.g., orange = red + yellow, green = blue + yellow, and purple/violet = red + blue). Intermediate colors are produced by mixing a primary and a secondary color (e.g., red-orange, yellow-orange, blue-green, yellow-green, blue-violet, or red-violet). Colors are arranged on the color wheel. Analogous colors are adjacent to each other on the wheel. Examples of analogous colors include yellow and orange, orange and red, blue and green, and green and yellow. Complementary colors are opposite each other on the color wheel. Examples of complementary colors include blue and orange, yellow and purple, and red and green. Mixing equal parts of two complementary colors produces brown. Blue and predominantly blue colors are cool. Red, yellow, and predominantly red/yellow colors are warm. Colors identify objects, evoke moods, and influence emotions.

## BALANCE

Balance refers to how visual weight is distributed in a work of visual art. In two-dimensional art like paintings, balance is the visual equilibrium among the painting's elements, which make the entire picture look balanced. Balance can be symmetrical (both sides are equal) or asymmetrical, with shapes and spaces that are unequal and/or unevenly distributed. This produces psychological rather than physical balance, creating tension and suggesting movement. Radial balance/symmetry uses images radiating from a center, such as wheel spokes or ripples around a pebble thrown into water. An example of balance is seen in the painting "Dressing for the Carnival" (1877) by Winslow Homer. The central figure of a carnival performer putting on his costume is the focal point. The performer is surrounded by two adult assistants and a group of fascinated children who are watching him. The shapes, values, and colors are balanced to produce overall visual equilibrium and unity (another organizing principle of art).

## VISUAL MOVEMENT

Artists create a visual sense of movement in paintings to direct the viewer's eyes. Direction is frequently toward a focal point or area within the painting. Artists can direct movement along lines, edges, shapes, and colors, but especially along parts with equal value (dark/light), which best facilitates the eyes' movement. For example, in "Liberation of the Peon" (1931), Diego Rivera depicts soldiers liberating a slave by cutting the ropes binding him while clothing his nakedness with a blanket or garment. Paths of movement in the painting all lead to the focal point of the knife cutting the ropes. (Emphasis, another art/design principle, is also seen in how the action of freeing the peon is made more important than the soldiers performing that action.) By painting all humans in the scene with their eyes focused on the slave, Rivera creates movement directing our view toward him. At the same time, he painted all horses with their eyes focused out at the viewer, drawing the viewer into the scene.

## USING EMPHASIS

Artists use the design principle of emphasis to call attention to particular elements in their works. Emphasis directs the viewer's focus to certain parts of a painting, and makes certain components of a work dominant. Emphasis can be achieved in art by emphasizing various design elements like value (light/dark), color, shape, line, etc. Artists also use contrast (e.g., contrasting values, colors, shapes, etc.) to create emphasis. To emphasize a focal area, a center of interest which focuses on the most important part of a painting, an artist can create visual emphasis through extreme contrasts of light and dark values. Strongly contrasting shapes and/or marked contrasts in other design elements also create visual emphasis. As an example of visual emphasis, in the painting "At the Moulin Rouge" (1892/1895), Henri de Toulouse-Lautrec emphasizes the focal area of a group of friends conversing in a cabaret through contrasting colors and values, as well as through movement directing the eye toward the group. His use of color, light, and shape also help create the scene's atmosphere.

## UNITY

One of the most important characteristics of a well-developed work of visual art is its visual unity. When we view a painting without unity, we may see a collection of disconnected parts that do not come together to form a whole. We may perceive it as fragmentary, disorganized, and incomplete. When an artist achieves visual unity, all of the elements in a painting appear to belong together. Unity affords paintings the quality of cohesion that makes them look and feel finished and complete. For example, in the painting "Starry Night" (1889), Vincent Van Gogh used his characteristic large, visible brush strokes in a swirly pattern throughout the landscape, providing visual unity through the texture, rhythm, pattern, and movement of the lines and shapes. He used predominantly cool colors (blues and bluish browns), providing unity through color. (He also provided emphasis by adding contrasting yellow stars.) The result is a unified painting whose elements work together, strongly conveying the atmosphere, mood, emotion, and story that the artist wanted to express.

## CONTRAST

Contrast refers to significant differences in the values (lights and darks), colors, textures, shapes, lines, and other elements of visual artworks. Visual contrast creates interest and excitement, and avoids monotony in art. For example, in the painting "Still Life with Apples and Peaches" (1905), Paul Cézanne combined all seven elements and all seven principles of design to create a unified composition. Among these, he used at least eight kinds of contrast: (1) unpatterned vs. intricately patterned surfaces (pattern contrast); (2) soft vs. hard/found edges (edge contrast); (3) dark vs. light vs. middle values (value contrast); (4) pure vs. muted/blended colors (intensity contrast); (5) cool vs. warm colors (temperature contrast); (6) textured vs. smooth surfaces (texture contrast); (7) organic vs. geometric shapes (shape contrast); and (8) large vs. small objects/shapes (size contrast).

## PATTERN

Pattern is the organized or random repetition of elements. Music is made up of sound patterns. Visual patterns often appear in nature. Artists frequently create works featuring repeated designs that produce patterns inspired by those seen in the natural world. Visual art is enhanced by pattern, which enriches surface interest to augment visual excitement. For example, in "Numbers in Color" (1958-59), the artist Jasper Johns created a regular pattern by assembling 11 rows of 11 stacked rectangles each. He painted various numerical digits from 0 to 9 within most of the rectangles. He made these numbers look irregular by irregularly distributing, varying, and applying the colors he used. Many patterned paintings do not include a focal point or area. This often makes them look

70

more like designs—even when they include recognizable images—than portraits, landscapes, still-lifes, or other types of paintings that do not have such repetitive patterning.

## PITCH, TEMPO, AND RHYTHM IN THE MUSICAL ARTS

Pitch is the frequency of a sound, such as a musical note. We hear high/middle/low frequency sound waves as high/middle/low pitched sounds. Various pitches are combined in musical compositions to create variety. A series of connected notes of different pitches creates a melody. Sounding (playing/singing) several pitches simultaneously and combining them produces harmonies and chords. Connected series of harmonies/chords in turn create harmonic/chord progressions. Tempo is the speed of music. Fast tempo can evoke happiness, excitement, fear, anger, or urgency. Slow tempo can evoke serenity, grandeur, solemnity, sadness, or ominousness. Musical compositions commonly direct the tempo using terms like andante (walking speed), adagio (slow), allegro (happy/quick), lento (slow), largo (expansively slow), etc. Rhythm includes the overall beat/time signature (number of beats per measure) and the variations among note lengths that produce patterns (e.g., legato describes smoothly connected series of notes, while staccato describes sharply disconnected notes that are cut short and sounded separately). Composers combine pitch, tempo, and rhythm in music to create atmosphere and mood, and to evoke emotion in listeners. They also arrange these elements to construct/recall musical themes/motifs within compositions.

# Praxis Practice Test

## Language and Literacy

**1. Children develop phonological awareness:**

    a. Only through direct training given by adults.
    b. Only naturally, through exposure to language.
    c. Via both natural exposure and direct training.
    d. Via neither incidental exposure nor instruction.

**2. Young children are more likely to respond to analogies in stories than to metaphors because**

    a. They are old enough to understand the abstract thinking and symbolism that analogies express
    b. The ability to understand the kinds of abstraction expressed in metaphors is not developed until later in childhood
    c. They can apply the concepts expressed in analogies to their own daily lives, but metaphors do not compare things that children are familiar with
    d. Metaphors and symbols are usually found only in books that children find boring because of their abstractions

**3. Young children's skills in phonological awareness are focused on:**

    a. Morphologies.
    b. Speech sounds.
    c. Word meanings.
    d. Word sequence.

**4. Which of the following is the earliest phonological feature to be independently recognizable in a typically developing child?**

    a. Syllables
    b. Alliteration
    c. Rhyming
    d. Letter-sound relationships

**5. Which of the following has research found most predictive of children's future long-term literacy performance?**

    a. Their scores on standardized intelligence tests
    b. Their family's relative socioeconomic status
    c. Their phonological and phonemic awareness
    d. Their early knowledge of vocabulary words

**6. What statement is accurate regarding normally developing oral language in children?**

    a. There is a considerable range of ages within normal individual growth.
    b. There are no individual differences among developmental milestones.
    c. Individual children achieve oral language milestones at specified ages.
    d. Individual children all develop spoken language skills at the same rates.

**7. To support EC language development, experts advise which of the following teacher practices?**

    a. Asking children linear or one-way questions
    b. Doing most of the talking in their classrooms
    c. Focusing on durations of verbal interactions
    d. Asking children more open-ended questions

**8. A student learning English as a second language (ESL) who has limited comprehension of English and can speak one- to two-word English answers, essential English words, present-tense English verbs, and some familiar English phrases is in which stage of second-language acquisition?**

    a. Preproduction
    b. Early Production
    c. Speech Emergence
    d. Intermediate Fluency

**9. A child who omits, substitutes, or distorts certain speech sounds beyond the usual age-range norms is most likely to have:**

    a. An articulation disorder.
    b. A type of voice disorder.
    c. One specific type of aphasia.
    d. Delayed language development.

**10. A four-year-old child who does not correctly or clearly produce the speech sounds /r/ and /s/:**

    a. Likely has delayed language development.
    b. Likely has normal articulatory development.
    c. Likely has some degree of hearing impairment.
    d. Likely needs early intervention for stuttering.

**11. The Alphabetic Principle is *best* defined as the concept that:**

    a. The letters of the alphabet are arranged in a specific sequence.
    b. The letters of the alphabet are combined to spell various words.
    c. The letters of the alphabet represent corresponding phonemes.
    d. The letters of the alphabet are used to create matching sounds.

**12. Which is true about instruction to improve preschoolers' alphabetic knowledge as needed?**

    a. Teachers should give only explicit instruction in isolated letter-sound matches.
    b. Teachers should only integrate letter-sound correspondences into curriculum.
    c. Teachers should provide opportunities for practice, but not isolated instruction.
    d. Teachers should combine explicit instruction, integration, and ways to practice.

**13. What is true about teaching ESL students English-language reading, including alphabetic knowledge?**

    a. Formal instruction in a second language can accelerate students' acquisition of English.
    b. Teachers should require ESL students to master each curriculum element consecutively.
    c. Providing students with linguistic activities meaningful to them promotes ESL acquisition.
    d. Letter-to-sound correspondences are the same across languages, so they transfer easily.

**14. Which of these is accurate regarding young children's development of print awareness?**

   a. The most common age for children to develop print awareness is between five and seven years.
   b. Research finds that four-year-olds are likely to acquire print concepts before word concepts.
   c. Preschoolers who attain print literacy skills are no more likely to read better at later ages.
   d. Print awareness is knowing that print has meaning, but not necessarily its form/function.

**15. The Interactive Book Reading teaching method promotes early literacy development and reading comprehension by incorporating all EXCEPT which of these strategies?**

   a. Curriculum-embedded assessments
   b. The 3S strategy (See, Show, and Say)
   c. Asking the students "Wh-" questions
   d. The Expanded Book Reading strategy

**16. Which of the following is true about the 3N (Notice, Nudge, Narrate) instructional strategy for developing early childhood literacy?**

   a. It does not incorporate any informal assessment of literacy levels.
   b. It uses scaffolding to promote further literacy skills development.
   c. It is a strategy that does not integrate any reflective components.
   d. This strategy is not found adaptable to games for young children.

**17. Which of the following reading comprehension strategies is *most* applicable to differentiating between homonyms without knowing their exact spellings?**

   a. Pictures
   b. Phonics
   c. Context
   d. Grammar

**18. Which of these is an example of attributes to seek in good children's literature?**

   a. Stable story characters who do not change
   b. Books featuring overtly moralistic themes
   c. Concise summaries of race/gender types
   d. Original yet believable plot constructions

**19. Which genre of children's literature is most likely to begin "Once upon a time..." and conclude with a happy ending?**

   a. Modern fantasy
   b. Picture books
   c. Traditional
   d. Poetry books

**20. Which of these is true regarding early signs of reading difficulties in young children?**

   a. A child's inability to form rhymes is not a concern, as long as s/he can identify rhymes.
   b. A child's inability to separate words into individual phonemes can indicate a problem.
   c. A child's inability to blend individual phonemes to form words is not a sign of trouble.
   d. A child's inability to count word syllables or spell new words phonetically is immaterial.

**21. Which of the following is accurate regarding conversational vs. academic English for ESL students?**
   a. Conversational English is not as cognitively demanding of ESLs as academic English.
   b. Conversational English deficits are the causes for ESL academic underachievement.
   c. Conversational English is harder for ESL students to develop than academic English.
   d. Conversational English takes the same time for ESLs to develop as academic English.

**22. Of the following activities that promote building vocabulary for young children, which one is *most* dependent on the teacher?**
   a. Repeatedly singing the same familiar song over and over
   b. Reciting the same familiar rhymes and chants repeatedly
   c. Listening to repeated readings of the same favorite story
   d. A word wall in the classroom to illustrate words/concepts

**23. Which of the following is true regarding children's reading fluency?**
   a. The lack of reading fluency is always due to word-decoding deficits.
   b. Children's motivation to read is unaffected by their reading fluency.
   c. Some children need only more reading practice to develop fluency.
   d. Fluency has equal impact on school performance at all grade levels.

**24. Which of these is an indication that a child has problems with reading comprehension?**
   a. The child wonders about why the characters in a story did some things.
   b. The child can tell how a story s/he read ended, but cannot explain why.
   c. The child makes predictions about what will happen next in a narrative.
   d. The child associates things in the reading with things in his/her own life.

**25. Regarding student problems that teachers may observe which can indicate dyslexia, which is true?**
   a. Dyslexic students perform worse on objective tests than their IQ and knowledge.
   b. Students with dyslexia typically have more trouble reading long than short words.
   c. Students who have dyslexia lack fluidity, but fare much better with rote memory.
   d. Dyslexic students have equal trouble understanding words in isolation or context.

**26. Concerning spelling, what statement is correct about how children learn?**
   a. Children must be taught spelling patterns as they will not learn them incidentally.
   b. Children who know basic spelling rules can deduce spellings for words they hear.
   c. Children may be able to spell words, but this does not mean they can read them.
   d. Children's reading and writing skills promote spelling, but the reverse is not true.

**27. According to linguists, what do invented spellings by young children best signify?**
   a. Children who invent spellings lack phonemic and phonetic awareness.
   b. Children's selections of phonetic spellings are due to adult influences.
   c. Inventing spellings for words is evidence of phonetic comprehension.
   d. Diverse children choosing the same phonetic spellings is just chance.

**28. In which stage of writing development do children understand that written forms symbolize meanings?**

- a. Scribbling and drawing
- b. Letters
- c. Letters and spaces
- d. Letter-like forms and shapes

**29. According to literacy experts, what is true about student writing for various purposes and audiences?**

- a. The primary purpose of student writing is expressing their ideas, thoughts, and emotions.
- b. The primary purpose of student writing is persuading their readers to agree/believe them.
- c. Improving student reading skills improves their writing skills, but not the other way around.
- d. Improving student writing skills as well as their reading skills improves their learning ability.

**30. In the POWER instructional strategy for teaching students the writing process, the P stands for:**

- a. Purpose
- b. Program
- c. Planning
- d. Partners

**31. One simple rating scale for assessing young children's early writing (Clay, 1993) divides skills into three areas: Language Level, Message Quality, and Directional Principles. Which of the following achievements falls into the Message Quality category?**

- a. The child can write two related sentences with punctuation.
- b. The child attempts to set down his/her own ideas in writing.
- c. The child can write a story with paragraphs and two themes.
- d. The child writes showing correct spacing between the words.

**32. Which of these correctly shows the normal developmental sequence of children's writing with regard to directional principles?**

- a. No knowledge; partial knowledge; reverses the direction; correct direction; correct spacing
- b. No knowledge; reverses the direction; partial knowledge; correct spacing; correct direction
- c. No knowledge; partial knowledge; correct spacing; reverses the direction; correct direction
- d. No knowledge; reverses the direction; correct direction; correct spacing; partial knowledge

**33. Regarding the standard conventions for written English when evaluating student writing, which of the following reflects the function of writing rather than its form?**

- a. The length of the student's composition
- b. Appropriate content in the composition
- c. Word usage in a student's composition
- d. The spelling in a student's composition

**34. Of the following writing examples, which one reflects an error in grammar?**

a. "She is without a doubt the very best freind I have ever had in my life."
b. "He said we should wait two hours, we waited two hours and returned."
c. "A great animal lover, his pets included dogs, cats, horses, and chickens."
d. "They were traveling South at first, but later in the trip they went West."

**35. Which of the following is most accurate about teacher strategies to promote young children's motivation to write?**

a. Children's enthusiasm is sustained by sticking with the same writing activities.
b. Children are less motivated to write about subjects that are familiar to them.
c. Children display greater writing motivation with predictable, routine activities.
d. Children are more motivated to participate in activities that they find exciting.

**36. In selecting literature for children, the most important first step a teacher should perform is to evaluate**

a. Whether the characters are interesting
b. Whether the plots are appealing
c. Class composition and preferences
d. The reading level of the material

# Mathematics

**37. Regarding the relationship of cognitive problem-solving skills to mathematics, which of these is true?**

a. Problem-solving skills inform mathematical thinking but not social skills.
b. Developing problem-solving skills aids math rather than language skills.
c. Students apply logical reasoning to solve every day and novel problems.
d. Children must be taught to have interest in solving everyday problems.

**38. Which of the following correctly describes a characteristic of students with effective problem-solving skills?**

a. Students develop hypotheses via repeated trial-and-error tests.
b. Students have developed demonstrated skills for self-regulation.
c. Students are cautious in solving problems and avoid taking a risk.
d. Students quickly switch to another problem if their solution fails.

**39. Which of these is correct about mental math games adults can initiate with young children to promote their problem-solving skills for learning math?**

a. Adults should always use concrete objects within oral story problems.
b. Adults should plan mental math games to adhere to child grade levels.
c. Adults should always keep problems simple with only whole numbers.
d. Adults should always tell young children correct answers to questions.

**40. To support children's development of reasoning skills for comprehending and applying early math and science concepts, which of these is the best adult behavior?**

a. Asking children "why?" questions and waiting until they find the expected answers
b. Asking children "why?" questions and disregarding both expected and real answers
c. Asking children "why?" questions and requiring them to answer them immediately
d. Asking children "why?" questions, giving time to think, and listening to the answers

**41. Which of these is true about children's transition from intuitive thinking to formal math education?**

    a. Children do not use mathematical thinking until they begin their formal school education.

    b. Children may see math as a set of rules and procedures, not as practical problem solving.

    c. Children will automatically apply their formal math learning to useful solutions in real life.

    d. Children are less likely to see connections between math and life using concrete objects.

**42. What is the most effective way to facilitate children's comprehension of mathematics?**

    a. To preserve mathematics as a discipline separate from other academic subjects and everyday life

    b. To allow children to find their own activities applying math rather than providing activities for them

    c. To help them connect and apply common math rules to many different life activities and processes

    d. To ask/answer questions and explain during formal math lessons, not confusing math with real life

**43. Which of the following is true regarding children's development of the concept of symbolic representation?**

    a. When young children engage in make-believe and pretend play, this is symbolic representation.

    b. Children do not develop this ability until they are old enough to engage in fully abstract thinking.

    c. Children first show this concept by reading, writing, and connecting written with spoken language.

    d. When young children first begin counting on their fingers, they have not yet developed this concept.

**44. Suppose that a child in a preschool learning center enjoys sorting different rocks by color. Which of the following teacher practices is the best example of emphasis on connecting the informal math activity with formal math vocabulary?**

    a. Telling the child s/he is classifying the rocks

    b. Asking the child how s/he is sorting the rocks

    c. Asking after s/he finishes other ways to sort

    d. These all exemplify the vocabulary emphasis

**45. Which of these is true about having an awareness of patterns and relationships in the real world?**

    a. Our understanding the basic structure of things is uninformed by it.

    b. It helps us understand series of events, but not predict future ones.

    c. It is unrelated to our basic feeling of confidence in the environment.

    d. It increases our self-efficacy about interacting with our environment.

**46. The property of numbers that states that 1 + 3 is the same as 3 + 1 is called**

    a. Associative

    b. Distributive

    c. Inverse

    d. Commutative

**47. Which of the following is most accurate regarding young children's development of numeracy skills?**

    a. Young children typically learn all of the number names before they learn to count.
    b. Young children typically learn to name all of the numbers and count simultaneously.
    c. Young children typically learn to count before they have learned all number names.
    d. Young children typically learn these two numeracy skills in individually varying order.

**48. What is a correct statement about the development of number sense in young children?**

    a. Children with developed number sense can count forward, but cannot necessarily count backward.
    b. Counting ability, number familiarity, and a good number sense enable children to add and subtract.
    c. Children who have developed number sense can break numbers down, but not reassemble them.
    d. Being able to identify relationships between/among numbers is an ability outside of number sense.

**49. For three days, Mr. Hanson had his students keep track of how many times each of them used a pencil during the school day. What is the best kind of graph to use to display these data?**

    a. Bar graph
    b. Circle graph
    c. Pictograph
    d. Line graph

**50. Which of the following would be most effective to help young children learn geometry?**

    a. Giving them hands-on activities manipulating concrete objects
    b. Giving the earliest geometric theorems for them to memorize
    c. Giving them everyday life activities only after they learn basics
    d. Giving them instructions for drawing geometric shape diagrams

**51. Of the following, what statement is correct regarding practice in measurement for young children?**

    a. Measurement is exclusively a formal method for quantifying sizes, time durations, weights, etc.
    b. Measurement is for both formal quantification and recognizing and finding real-life relationships.
    c. Measurement can only be accomplished by young children with standard measurement devices.
    d. Measurement practice for young children is unlikely to help them in learning about comparisons.

**52. Which of these is correct regarding young children and the measurement of time?**

    a. Young children typically develop an understanding of the abstract concept of time very early.

    b. Adults should not refer to periods of time with young children before they understand them.

    c. Using activities involving counting allows children to generalize these to the counting of time.

    d. Adults can say "yesterday, today, tomorrow" with young children and they will understand it.

**53. Regarding young children's early comprehension of fractions, which of these is accurate?**

    a. Children must know how many parts a unit is divided into, but not what comprises the unit.

    b. Children must know what makes a whole unit, but not into how many pieces it was divided.

    c. Children must know how many pieces a unit is divided into, but not if they are of equal size.

    d. Children must know what a whole unit is, how many parts there are, and if part sizes match.

**54. Of the following, which is prerequisite for young children to understand before they can engage in accurately estimating basic measurements of quantities?**

    a. Knowledge of math vocabulary words indicating estimation

    b. Knowledge of how to make predictions that are appropriate

    c. Knowledge of how to achieve estimates that are reasonable

    d. Knowledge of what relative quantities and comparisons are

**55. Which of these is/are most representative of using statistics in everyday life to predict probabilities?**

    a. An actuarial table in an insurance company

    b. A weather forecast for the chances of rain

    c. A chart comparing results of interventions

    d. Answers (A) and (B) represent probability

**56. A teacher asks ten preschoolers to choose their favorite among four colors of foil stars. Five children pick gold; three choose silver; two select blue; and one picks red. The teacher then helps the student to stick the stars onto a paper chart with a separate row for each color:**

GOLD ★★★★★

SILVER ★★★

BLUE ★★

RED ★

**This activity supports which of the following early mathematics skills?**

    a. Determining various properties of figures

    b. Applying mathematical formulas to shapes

    c. Collecting, organizing, and displaying data

    d. Intuitively identifying probability concepts

**57. A teacher presents this figure and asks the class how many different rectangles they can find in it.**

**Which student response is correct?**

a. Andrea's answer, "Only one."
b. Billy's answer, "There are four."
c. Charlie's answer, "I found ten."
d. Darlene's answer, "I count five."

**58. Which of the following statements is an example of using ordinal numbers?**

a. "I am four years old and my brother Timmy is two years old."
b. "I sit at the first table for lunch and my sister sits at the third."
c. "I play on the junior soccer team. My shirt says number six."
d. "Two-thirds of my math class are boys and one-third is girls."

**59. A group of five- and six-year-olds watch a teacher demonstrate measuring things with a standard ruler. Some students want to know why the teacher aligns the number 0 on the ruler with the first edge of an object, instead of starting with the number 1 as they do when they count. Which choice is the best answer for the teacher to give?**

a. To tell them this is how the teacher learned to do it in school
b. To tell them this is how we include the first inch on the ruler
c. To tell them this is how we can use the most space on rulers
d. To tell them this is how we follow standard ruler convention

**60. Which level of shape perception do young children typically develop first?**

a. Recognizing shapes
b. Naming the shapes
c. Analysis of shapes
d. All develop at once

**61. A teacher regularly integrates math into everyday EC activities. By asking young children to help at snack time by putting one snack on each plate, which math skill is the teacher primarily engaging?**

a. 1:1 correspondence
b. Practice in counting
c. Shapes recognition
d. Comparison of size

**62. How can an EC teacher best facilitate children's development of math communication and literacy?**

a. By asking the children questions
b. By observing children's behaviors
c. By lecturing to model language use
d. By having children write about math

**63. Preschoolers' development of spatial awareness will later support their comprehension of which areas of math the most?**

    a.  Arithmetic and algebra

    b.  Geometry and physics

    c.  Arithmetic and physics

    d.  Geometry and algebra

**64. Of the following, which preschool activity is most related to learning 1:1 correspondence?**

    a.  Being able to name all printed numbers on sight

    b.  The ability to count numbers both up and down

    c.  Counting out pennies to match a written number

    d.  These all relate the same to 1:1 correspondence

**65. Which of the following is a rational number?**

    a.  The value of pi ($\pi$)

    b.  Square root of 2 ($\sqrt{2}$)

    c.  Any decimal number

    d.  9,731,245/42,754,021

# Social Studies

**66. In EC development in the area of interpersonal interactions, which do children typically develop first?**

    a.  Autonomy/independence

    b.  Trusting/mistrusting others

    c.  A sense of initiative or guilt

    d.  Make-believe/pretending

**67. What is true about instructing children in conflict resolution skills and processes?**

    a.  Conflict resolution can be taught to children who are as young as eighteen months.

    b.  Children can only understand these concepts at school ages (six years and up).

    c.  Conflict resolution instruction has never been attempted with young children.

    d.  Children taught conflict mediation/resolution are unlikely to generalize these.

**68. Of these four parenting styles described by psychologists, which is considered the ideal?**

    a.  Authoritative

    b.  Authoritarian

    c.  Permissive

    d.  Uninvolved

**69. According to family systems theory, when one member of a family is consistently identified as the family peacemaker and another is viewed as the family clown, these most reflect which system component?**

    a.  Boundaries

    b.  Roles

    c.  Rules

    d.  Equilibrium

**70. A child whose family comes from a collectivist culture is most likely to value:**
   a. Competition.
   b. Independence.
   c. Cooperation.
   d. Uniqueness.

**71. A family moves to America from another country with a very different culture. They discard their native cultural practices and adopt American customs. This is an example of:**
   a. Accommodation
   b. Adaptation
   c. Acculturation
   d. Assimilation

**72. Which of the following is most accurate about cultural competence in educational professionals?**
   a. Hiring language interpreters and translators will assure cultural competence.
   b. Hiring educational staff with racial diversity will ensure cultural competence.
   c. Hiring highly culturally self-aware educators will create cultural competence.
   d. Hiring these plus educator communication skills creates cultural competence.

**73. Research comparing American Latino and White parent beliefs has found that:**
   a. Most White parents believe that children's learning capacities are set at birth.
   b. Most White and Latino parents share the same beliefs about learning capacity.
   c. Most Latino parents believe children's learning capacities are fixed from birth.
   d. Most Latino parents highly value early intervention and stimulation of learning.

**74. Which statement is most accurate regarding variations among culturally diverse U.S. parents in whether or how often they read to their young children?**
   a. Parents who succeeded despite not being read to as children value reading to children even more.
   b. Some cultures with oral traditions tell stories and sing to their children more than reading to them.
   c. Educators can easily influence parents whose culture does not value/prioritize reading to children.
   d. Parents not seeing school readiness and success as benefits can still be taught to read to children.

**75. Which statement is true of findings about culturally diverse parental views of child development milestones in America?**
   a. Parents in America from different cultures expect their children to reach milestones at different ages.
   b. Anglo, Filipino, and Puerto Rican parents in America differ in age expectations only for sleeping lone.
   c. Anglo, Filipino, and Puerto Rican parents in America expect children to eat solid food at the same age.
   d. The only age expectation shared by all parents is when their children should sleep through the night.

**76. Land is typically more expensive in urban areas than in rural areas. Which geography concept does this reflect?**

    a. Location
    b. Distance
    c. Pattern
    d. Interaction

**77. As used in geographical maps, which of the following is a synonym for the term *latitude?***

    a. Longitude
    b. Parallel
    c. Meridian
    d. Coordinate

**78. Which of the following is correct regarding common types of graphs?**

    a. A pie chart shows differences in quantities over time.
    b. A bar graph can compare quantities but not over time.
    c. A line graph clarifies how amounts change over time.
    d. A number column makes patterns and trends clearer.

**79. Of these materials, which can teachers use to help students develop chronological thinking?**

    a. Only history books can be used for this.
    b. Biographies can also serve this function.
    c. Historical literature can be used for this.
    d. These are all good chronology materials.

**80. To teach citizenship at the EC level, what purposes of laws and rules should teachers help young children to understand?**

    a. People who are employed in positions of authority wield unlimited powers.
    b. Individual citizens determine their own responsibilities separately from laws.
    c. Individuals and groups make up our government to create and enforce laws.
    d. Life and society are unpredictable, insecure and disorderly, despite any laws.

# Science

**81. Young children develop many basic science concepts through everyday activities. Of the following, which activity is most related to the development of measurement concepts?**

    a. Fitting wooden pegs into holes with matching shapes in a toy
    b. Pouring sand from one container into a differently sized one
    c. Seeing how many coins they have accrued in their piggy bank
    d. Separating toys into piles of cars, trucks, animals, people, etc.

**82. Which is the best definition of an informal learning experience for learning basic science concepts?**

    a. A child chooses what to do, and an adult provides some intervention
    b. A child chooses what to do spontaneously without adult intervention
    c. A child engages in an activity which is chosen and directed by an adult
    d. A child engages in a group activity assigned by the preschool teacher

**83. Of the following actions, which best represents the science process skill of Inference?**

    a. Formulating new hypotheses based on experimental results

    b. Finding patterns and meaning in the results of experiments

    c. Identifying properties of things/situations using the senses

    d. Reporting experimental results and conclusions to others

**84. Which of the following gases is known as a compound gas?**

    a. Oxygen

    b. Nitrogen

    c. Ammonia

    d. Hydrogen

**85. When we look at a straw in a glass of water, the straw appears broken or bent at the waterline. This appearance is a function of:**

    a. Scattering.

    b. Absorption.

    c. Reflection.

    d. Refraction.

**86. Which statement is correct regarding the phenomenon of magnetism?**

    a. Opposite poles of magnets repel each other.

    b. The like poles of magnets attract each other.

    c. Magnets can attract/repel without touching.

    d. Magnets work beyond their magnetic fields.

**87. Heat is transmitted through solid materials via:**

    a. Conduction.

    b. Convection.

    c. Radiation.

    d. All three.

**88. Newton's First Law of Motion states that:**

    a. An object at rest tends to stay at rest unless an opposing force changes this.

    b. An object stays at rest or in motion unless/until an opposing force changes it.

    c. An object in motion tends to stay in motion until an opposing force changes it.

    d. For every action that take place, there is an equal and opposite reaction to it.

**89. Which of the following will not conduct sound waves?**

    a. solids

    b. liquids

    c. gases

    d. vacuum

**90. Which type of rock typically forms on the surface of the earth in cumulative layers?**

    a. Igneous

    b. Obsidian

    c. Metamorphic

    d. Sedimentary

**91. Which organisms depend *most* on light to survive?**

    a.  Undersea plants
    b.  Mammalians
    c.  Land plants
    d.  Humans

**92. Which of the following have a simple life cycle, without a metamorphosis?**

    a.  Frogs
    b.  Newts
    c.  Grasshoppers
    d.  Human beings

**93. Of the following insects, which undergo a complete metamorphosis during their life cycle?**

    a.  Mosquitos
    b.  Butterflies
    c.  Dragonflies
    d.  Grasshoppers

# Health and Physical Education

**94. The American Recovery and Reinvestment Act (2009) includes funding or the U.S. Dept. of Health and Human Services to prevent chronic disease. This initiative targets which of the following as the most preventable causes of disability and death?**

    a.  Obesity and tobacco use
    b.  Alcohol and tobacco use
    c.  Alcohol and drug abuse
    d.  Obesity and diabetes

**95. Which statement is true about children and environmental health risks?**

    a.  Children's body systems are more robust and resilient than adults' are.
    b.  Children are liable to be more vulnerable to environmental health risks.
    c.  Children take in fewer toxins from the air, water, and food than adults.
    d.  Children's normal behaviors expose them to fewer toxins than adults'.

**96. A part of which of these human body systems regulates the body temperature?**

    a.  Lymphatic
    b.  Circulatory
    c.  Integumentary
    d.  Musculoskeletal

**97. Which of the following systems is responsible for producing the white blood cells in the body?**

    a.  The integumentary system
    b.  The nervous system
    c.  The circulatory system
    d.  The lymphatic system

**98. Prenatal, infant, and child motor development progresses from the head down. This is known as:**

   a. Cephalocaudal development
   b. Proximodistal development
   c. Mediolateral development
   d. Intellectual development

**99. Which of the following is true about young children's physical activity?**

   a. Children's motor skills generally develop later than their language skills.
   b. Attempting and succeeding at physical challenges enhances self-efficacy.
   c. Physical activity develops children's physical rather than cognitive skills.
   d. Only language and arts skills can give children means of self-expression.

**100. Which of these is true about the National Association for Sport and Physical Education (NASPE)'s national standards for physical education?**

   a. They include learning and executing physical activities rather than concepts.
   b. They include conducting physical activities rather than showing motor skills.
   c. They include understanding concepts as well as engaging in physical activity.
   d. They include valuing physical and personal but not social benefits of activity.

**101. The World Health Organization (WHO) recommends at least _____ of moderate to vigorous physical activity for children aged five to seventeen.**

   a. 15 minutes a day
   b. 30 minutes a day
   c. 1 hour every day
   d. 1 hour per week

# Creative and Performing Arts

**102. Of the following, which is correct regarding arts education in early childhood?**

   a. EC teachers should focus on assigning separate art activities so children realize art's importance.
   b. EC teachers enhance learning and comprehension by integrating art into the overall curriculum.
   c. EC teachers are told by many state standards to integrate art into units but not whole curricula.
   d. EC teachers who assign art process activities should be giving children any rules or steps in advance.

**103. An EC teacher gives children an art activity of illustrating and labeling plants or animals by name that they learned about in a science unit. This best exemplifies which learning application of art?**

   a. Using art to build their language skills and vocabularies
   b. Developing skills of color recognition and discrimination
   c. Developing awareness of line, shape, color, and texture
   d. Using art to express feelings and thoughts, and tell stories

**104. When planning an art project or activity for young children, which should the teacher do first?**

    a. Construct a simple prototype of the intended product.
    b. Establish which particular concept s/he wants to teach.
    c. Determine learning objectives for the children to meet.
    d. Identify teacher objectives for planning and instruction.

**105. Which of these statements is true about the context of a given work of art?**

    a. An artwork's context and its function are separate, unrelated aspects.
    b. The context of a given work of art is primarily determined by the artist.
    c. An artwork's function relies on context which is half artist, half viewer.
    d. The context of a given work of art is primarily determined by a viewer.

**106. While students are engaged in creating their own artworks, their teacher shows them other students' work. The teacher's doing this facilitates:**

    a. Generalization/transfer from the creation process to the response process.
    b. Generalization/transfer from the response process to the creation process.
    c. Generalization/transfer from an analysis process to an interpreting process.
    d. Generalization/transfer from the interpretation into the evaluation process.

**107. Which of the following is defined as a primary color?**

    a. Orange
    b. Yellow
    c. Green
    d. Purple

**108. The sound wave frequency of a musical note is its:**

    a. Tempo
    b. Melody
    c. Pitch
    d. Rhythm

**109. The waltz is traditionally associated most with which time signature?**

    a. 2/2
    b. 2/4
    c. 4/4
    d. 3/4

**110. Among art's organizing principles, Beethoven's *Symphony No. 5* makes striking use of which principle related specifically to its main theme?**

    a. Movement
    b. Repetition
    c. Contrast
    d. Pattern

# General Pedagogy

**111. Which of these is NOT one of the major personality structures proposed by Sigmund Freud in his psychoanalytic theory of development?**

   a. Id
   b. Ego
   c. Libido
   d. Superego

**112. Piaget coined the term "schema" to describe:**

   a. Mental constructs for individual objects.
   b. Mental concepts of categories or classes.
   c. Mental programs only for motor actions.
   d. Mental ideas governing inborn reflexes.

**113. When a student is able to consider whether an information source is reputable, has been proven objectively, and is accepted by experts in its discipline, which element of critical thinking does the student demonstrate?**

   a. Evaluating supporting evidence
   b. Judging the quality of material
   c. Distinguishing fact from opinion
   d. Finding evidence/no evidence

**114. Regarding the three basic temperament types identified by psychologists in infants, which of these is true?**

   a. There is no clear majority among infants having one of the types.
   b. The majority of babies are found to be of Difficult temperament.
   c. The majority of infants are found to be Slow to Warm Up types.
   d. The majority of infants are found to have the Easy temperament.

**115. Which of the following correctly reflects Adler's theory of birth order's influences on personality development?**

   a. The youngest children in families have no features in common with only children.
   b. Twins are identical in activity and/or strength and parents perceive them as equal.
   c. Some "babies" of the family grow to make grandiose plans, which never succeed.
   d. Adler never noted any differences between twins as to personality development.

**116. In Maslow's theory, which needs are at the base of the pyramid?**

   a. Self-actualizing
   b. Physiological
   c. Security
   d. Esteem

**117. According to Carl Rogers, a child who relies primarily on external locus of control demonstrates:**

   a. Incongruence
   b. Conditions of worth
   c. Conditional positive self-regard
   d. Unconditional positive regard

**118. Of the following, which is correct about considerations in arranging indoor learning environments to fit with curriculum planning for toddlers and preschoolers?**

    a. Rooms should be arranged to limit activities to certain areas.
    b. The floors in all the rooms should be covered with carpeting.
    c. The rooms should be organized to enable different activities.
    d. Math and science activities should be in one classroom area.

**119. A teacher tells a class that anybody who gets 100 percent on the next quiz will be excused from doing homework for that day. According to behaviorist terminology relative to motivation theory, this incentive is an example of what technique?**

    a. Positive reinforcement
    b. Primary reinforcement
    c. Negative reinforcement
    d. Secondary reinforcement

**120. In indoor EC learning environments, which of the following is most related to providing for children's privacy needs?**

    a. Adult laps for cuddling
    b. Pillows and soft upholstery
    c. Areas of floor with thick carpets
    d. Small inner rooms and partitions

# Answer Key and Explanations

## Language and Literacy

**1. C:** Children develop phonological awareness through a combination of incidental learning via being naturally exposed to language in their environments, and receiving direct instruction from adults. They do not develop it solely through one or the other, or neither.

**2. B:** The ability to understand the abstract concept expressed in metaphors is not developed until later in childhood. Analogies are easier for children to understand because they compare known items, whereas metaphors require abstract thinking.

**3. B:** Speech sounds or phonemes are the focus of phonological awareness skills, as well as the relationships of speech sounds to written language symbols. Morphologies (A) are the structural aspects of letters, syllables, and words that reflect grammatical changes. Word meanings (C) are called semantics, not morphology or phonology. Word sequences (D) or sentence structures are called syntax.

**4. C:** Phonological awareness skills are developed over the course of several years, and where there may be overlap in development, recognition of rhymes (C) comes rather early, between 2 and 3 years of age. Recognition of alliteration comes shortly thereafter, whereas syllables are recognizable between 3 and 6 years old. Phonic understanding is much more complex, as it requires a coordination between auditory and visual understanding.

**5. C:** Many educational research studies find that having strong phonological and phonemic awareness in early childhood is more predictive of later successful literacy performance than intelligence (A), socioeconomic status (B), or vocabulary knowledge (D) are.

**6. A:** Within normal development, individual children do vary (B) as to when they reach developmental milestones in spoken language. Due this variance, normal oral language development is represented in ranges rather than specific ages (C). In addition to developing at different ages within ranges, normally developing children also vary in the rates (D) at which they develop oral language skills.

**7. D:** Researchers advise EC teachers to ask children more open-ended questions, the kind that allow the children and the teacher to give two- and three-way responses in conversations, rather than the more common but less desirable practice of asking linear questions that demand one-way responses (A). They also criticize teachers' tendency to do most of the talking (B) in classrooms rather than encouraging children to use conversational language, which is preferable. Experts advise teachers not to focus only on the quantity of conversations (C), but equally on their quality.

**8. B:** Early Production, with the characteristics named, is the second stage of ESL acquisition. Preproduction (A), the first stage, involves no English speech; minimal listening comprehension; and the abilities to draw pictures of and/or point at objects represented by some English words. Speech Emergence (C) is the third stage, characterized by good English comprehension; English speech using simple sentences, but still showing pronunciation and grammatical errors; and frequently misunderstanding English-language jokes. Intermediate Fluency (D), the fourth stage, features excellent English listening comprehension and few spoken grammatical errors.

**9. A:** Articulation is the correct pronunciation of speech sounds (phonemes), and articulation disorders are characterized by incorrectly pronouncing one or multiple phonemes beyond the usual age range norms for the speech sound (age norms are older for more difficult sounds). Voice disorders (B) affect voice qualities like nasality, pitch, volume, and tone rather than pronunciation of specific phonemes. Aphasias (C) are cognitive language-processing disorders that affect language comprehension and/or production, e.g., word retrieval, grammatical sentence composition, etc. Delayed language development (D) falls behind normal developmental ranges for understanding and producing language, but not necessarily speech sounds.

**10. B:** The age norms for correctly pronouncing these most difficult of phonemes, /r/ and /s/, are around seven to eight years old. Thus a four-year-old who substitutes /w/ for /r/, lisps on /s/ or otherwise distorts it, or omits either/both of these sounds likely has normal development in speech articulation. Delayed language development (A) is not signaled by mispronouncing phonemes but by being significantly behind age norms for comprehending and constructing language. Hearing impairment (C) often causes misarticulations; however, errors in only two difficult phonemes when far below the age norms do not indicate it. Misarticulating phonemes is not a symptom of stuttering (D).

**11. C:** The best definition of the Alphabetic Principle is that the letters of the alphabet are symbols to represent the various phonemes (speech sounds) we use in our language. While it is true that the alphabet has a sequence (A), this does not define the Alphabetic Principle. The sequence serves as a master mnemonic to help us remember all the letters, but we could still identify letters and associate them with phonemes without it. Similarly, (B) is true but is not the definition. (D) is the reverse of the correct answer (sounds => letters, not letters => sounds).

**12. D:** Teachers' instructional plans for preschoolers with inadequate alphabetic knowledge should include NOT ONLY explicit instruction in isolated letter-sound correspondences (A); NOT ONLY curricular lessons and activities that integrate letter-sound relationships (B); and NOT ONLY regular opportunities for children to practice their newly developing alphabetic knowledge (C), but all of these together.

**13. C:** When teachers provide language-related activities for ESL students that are relevant to them personally, this is found to help them acquire English. Formal instruction does NOT speed up English acquisition (A): it can facilitate and inform the process and expand ESL students' knowledge, but because language learning is not linear, formal instruction will not make it happen faster. For this reason, teachers also should NOT require ESL students to master every individual curriculum element before starting another (B). Teachers must also realize that letter-sound correspondences are NOT the same across languages (D). For example, Spanish letters correspond better to their sounds than in English; therefore, native Spanish speakers are apt to be confused at the multiple sounds of many English letters/letter combinations (e.g., "-ough" as in *through, though, rough, ought, bough*).

**14. B:** Studies do show that although four-year-olds are unlikely to have mastered either print or word concepts, they may have learned many print concepts earlier than word concepts. The most common age for normally developing children to develop print awareness is between three and five years, not five and seven years (A). Studies show that preschoolers who attain print literacy skills ARE more likely to read better when they are older (C). Print awareness is defined as not only knowing that print has meaning, but also understanding the form and function of print (D).

**15. A:** Using curriculum-embedded assessments is another instructional strategy to enhance early literacy development and reading comprehension, but it is not included in Interactive Book

Reading. The Interactive Book Reading method incorporates three primary strategies: the 3S (See, Show, and Say) strategy (B); the strategy of asking "Wh-" questions (C); and the strategy of Expanded Book Reading (D).

**16. B:** The 3N strategy does use scaffolding, i.e., temporary support that the teacher provides to help young students achieve tasks at levels higher than their current literacy status. Scaffolding is gradually withdrawn as students become more proficient until they can achieve these tasks independently. 3N *does* incorporate informal assessment of literacy levels (A): the first, "Notice" step involves the teacher's noticing each individual student's current level of literacy skills. It *does* integrate reflection (C): the third, "Narrate" step involves the teacher's reflecting on what the student does. This strategy *is* adaptable to young children's games (D): various literacy games designed for young children apply the 3N strategy.

**17. C:** The most helpful strategy for discerning which of two homonyms (sound-alike words) is correct without knowing the spelling is its surrounding context of the sentence, paragraph, and/or book and subject matter. For example, "Mexico cedes land" and "Mexico seeds land" sound the same, but if the context continues "to the United States," the meaning of "cedes" applies. Pictures (A) help children identify unknown words rather than differentiate homonyms. Phonics (B) help students sound out unfamiliar words, not differentiate meanings. Grammar (D) can help when one homonym is a verb and the other a noun, for example; but "cedes" and "seeds" are the same part of speech with different meanings, so grammar alone does not help as much as context.

**18. D:** Good children's books should feature plots that are well-constructed, and are original but not incredible. Narrative books should feature story characters who are believable, which includes their changing (A) and growing as a result of their experiences like real people do, rather than staying the same throughout the story. Adults choosing children's literature should seek books with themes of value to children, but avoid books with overtly moralistic themes (B). Likewise they should avoid books that promote racial, gender, and other stereotypes (C).

**19. C:** These features are most characteristic of traditional literature, which has been adapted by authors from oral traditions including folklore, epics, fables, proverbs, and fairy tales. The modern fantasy (A) genre, which includes modern-day fairy tales and tells imaginative tales, may use traditional literature themes as its foundation, but is original writing by authors such as Hans Christian Andersen, Lewis Carroll, and E.B. White. Picture books (B) combine text and pictures, which help beginning students learn to read by supplementing words with illustrations. Poetry books (D) contain poems rather than prose writing.

**20. B:** If a young child cannot break down a word into its component phonemes, this represents a deficit in phonological and/or phonemic awareness, which will cause reading difficulties. Likewise, the inability to do the reverse and blend individual phonemes to form words (C) is a sign the child will have trouble reading. Young children with good phonological and phonemic awareness can both identify *and* form rhymes (A). To learn to read well, they should also be able to count the syllables in a word and use phonetic spellings (by sound) for new/unfamiliar words (D).

**21. A:** Conversational English is much *less* difficult (A) for ESL students to learn because it is much less demanding of them cognitively. Most often, academic underachievement in ESL students is caused by deficits in academic, not conversational English (B). The disparity in ease of developing these separate skill sets—basic, everyday-life interpersonal communication skills in conversational English vs. the complex-compound syntax and vocabularies specific to math, science, social studies, and other content areas in academic English—is apparent in the fact that while most ESL children develop conversational English within about two years of living in English-speaking settings, they take at least five to seven years to develop academic English (D).

**22. D:** A word wall uses visual illustrations of vocabulary words and the concepts they represent, and includes additional words, concepts, and pictures related to the main words and pictures to enrich vocabulary and relational thinking. The teacher would be most responsible for creating the word wall, using it in lessons/activities, and instructing/assisting young children in its use. The children themselves can and will repeatedly sing the same familiar song (A) and repeat the same rhymes and chants (B), which enhance vocabulary development for both native English-speaking and ESL students. Stories (C) may be read live by teachers, or readings may be recorded. Either way, the children play the same role of listening to repeated readings.

**23. C:** While *some* children's reading lacks fluency due to deficits in their word-decoding abilities, this is not *always* (A) the case: some children simply need more reading practice to develop fluency. Children's motivation to read (B) *is* affected by their reading fluency: when reading is laborious, children do not enjoy it and avoid reading; when reading is easy, children enjoy it and want to read. Fluency has much *greater* impact (D) on the performance of students in higher grades, when the volume of reading required of them in school is exponentially greater.

**24. B:** If a child can repeat the factual elements of how a story ended, but cannot explain why this ending occurred, this may show that the child cannot reason about cause and effect, logic, and sequencing in the material s/he has read; and/or lacks the expressive language skills to explain. Wondering about characters' reasons for their actions (A) indicates comprehension, not its lack: readers with good comprehension will speculate about character motivations, and will also try to predict future events in a book (C) before reading of them. Relating reading matter to one's own life (D) and pre-existing knowledge also does not indicate comprehension problems, but rather good reading comprehension.

**25. A:** Students with dyslexia tend to perform much worse than their intelligence and knowledge would indicate on objective formats like multiple-choice tests. They are likely to have *equal* amounts of difficulty with reading short function words (e.g., *an, on, in*) as with reading long, multisyllabic words (B). While they do have trouble with fluid thinking, e.g., thinking "on the spot" to produce spoken and/or written verbal responses, they also have equal difficulty with retaining and/or retrieving names, dates, random lists, phone numbers, and other information through rote memorization and recall (C). Students with dyslexia typically have more trouble understanding words in isolation than in context (D), because they rely on the surrounding context to comprehend word meanings.

**26. B:** Once children have learned the basic rules and principles for spelling in their native language, they can usually figure out how to spell words that are new to them when they hear them spoken. As children accrue experience in communicating with language, they notice basic patterns in letter combinations, syllables, common word roots, prefixes, suffixes, endings, etc., so much of their knowledge of spelling patterns comes through incidental learning (A). Also, children usually can read words that they can spell (C). Therefore, not only do their reading and writing skills support correct spelling, but reciprocally, good spelling skills also support children's reading and writing (D).

**27. C:** Linguists have found through research studies that not only do preschool children invent spellings for words before they have learned their actual spellings, but moreover, preschoolers from diverse backgrounds all choose the same phonetic spellings, at a rate higher than can be attributed to chance (D) or adult influences (B). The researchers have concluded that through these common invented, phonetic spellings, young children demonstrate comprehension—not a lack thereof (A)—of the phonetic characteristics of words, and of how conventional word spellings symbolize these characteristics.

**28. D:** Five stages identified in children's writing development are: Scribbling and drawing (A), wherein they hold crayons/pencils in their fists and explore line, space, and form; Letter-like forms and shapes (D), wherein they understand that written forms symbolize meanings and begin drawing circles, squares, and other shapes, drawing figures and asking parents what they "say." In the Letters (B) stage, children can form letter shapes, usually starting with consonants, and enjoy writing their own name initials. They only gradually develop understanding of the sounds represented by the letters. In the Letters and spaces (C) stage, children develop word concepts and space correctly between words. The fifth stage is Conventional writing and spelling, including correct punctuation and purposeful writing.

**29. D:** Research into literacy development reveals that improvement in students' writing skills improves their overall learning ability, just as improvement in their reading skills also does. Expressing ideas, thoughts, and feelings (A) is *one* purpose of student writing, but not the only or main one. Another purpose is persuasion of the reader audience to agree with the writer's point of view and/or believe the writer's assertions—again, not the only or main purpose (B), but one of various purposes. Research also finds not only that improving student reading skills improves their writing, but *also* that, reciprocally, improving student writing skills improves their reading (C).

**30. C:** POWER stands for Planning, Organization, Writing, Editing, and Rewriting. The first, Planning, step is particularly important because many students tend simply to plunge into writing without making any plans in advance for choosing a good topic, researching and/or reading on the topic, considering which information will appeal to the reader audience, and writing down all their ideas on the topic.

**31. B:** The category of Message Quality includes understanding the concepts of signs and symbols, of communicating a message; copying messages; repeating formulaic sentence patterns (e.g., "This is a...."); attempting to use writing to record one's own ideas; and successfully composing writing. Writing two related sentences with punctuation (A) and writing a story with paragraphs and two themes (C) are progressive levels of development falling into the Language Level category. Spacing correctly between written words (D) is a level of the Directional Principles category.

**32. A:** First, a child typically shows no knowledge of the correct direction in which to write (left-right, top-bottom in English); then partial knowledge, e.g., *either* left-right *or* top-bottom *or* moving from the upper right at the end of one line to the left for the next line; then reversed writing direction; then correct directionality; then correct direction plus correct spacing between words.

**33. B:** How appropriate the content of a student's composition is reflects function rather than form. Composition length (A), word usage (C), and spelling (D) in a student's composition are all reflections of the composition's form rather than its function.

**34. C:** This sentence contains the grammatical error of a misplaced modifier. The modifying phrase "a great animal lover" does NOT modify "his pets" but him (e.g., "A great animal lover, *he had* pets including...."). Choice (A) contains a spelling error: "friend" is misspelled. A common student error is to transpose vowel combinations like this. Choice (B) has a punctuation error: these two independent clauses should be separated by a semicolon, not a comma. (In this example, a colon would also be acceptable, but not a comma, which creates a run-on sentence.) Choice (D) has a capitalization error: "South" and "West" are only capitalized when used as names, e.g., "the wild West" or "the sunny South," but when used as directions are lowercase.

**35. D:** Educational experts find that children, like adults, are more motivated to participate in activities that are exciting to them than to engage in activities they find uninteresting or boring. They also advise that to sustain children's enthusiasm for writing, teachers should provide diverse writing activities rather than getting stuck in a predictable routine (C) of always using the same ones (A). They note that children's familiarity with the subject they write about increases their motivation rather than decreasing it (B).

**36. C:** Class composition and preferences. Before selecting literature for the classroom, the teacher needs to assess the class, considering where they are with their reading skills and what their current interests are. After determining these things, the teacher would next evaluate books that seem appropriate for this particular group of children in terms of plot, character, and reading level.

# Mathematics

**37. C:** Students apply logical reasoning to solve both usual, everyday problems and unusual, novel problems they encounter. Developing problem-solving skills not only helps students to think mathematically; it also develops their social skills (A) and language skills (B) when they collaborate to solve problems in math questions, in other school subjects, and in real life; and when they communicate, compare, and discuss their solutions. Children are naturally curious about how everyday problems can be solved: rather than having to teach them this interest (D), teachers can take advantage of this naturally existing motivation by asking them to propose problems; to propose solutions to problems and explain how they reached them; and asking questions about problems and solutions.

**38. B:** Emotional and behavioral self-regulation skills are important components of problem-solving abilities in students. Without these, students would not have the patience, persistence, and flexibility to keep trying alternative solutions if their first solution fails (D). Another characteristic of problem-solving behavior is to formulate hypotheses first and then test them for accuracy, not vice versa (A). An additional characteristic of good problem-solvers is to be willing to take reasonable risks (C).

**39. A:** Whether they actually introduce physical objects for the youngest children, or simply describe concrete objects in oral story problems, adults should always ask young children these in terms of concrete objects. For example, asking, "two + two = what?" may be too abstract; but asking, "If you have two grapes and I give you two more, how many will you have?" facilitates children's ability to manipulate numbers via seeing them as familiar items. Adults can start with favorite foods and then add problems using toys, cars, grocery items, etc. According to experts, adults should not restrict such games to grade levels (B): young children can address any scenario for which they can form mental images. Adults are also advised to include occasional harder problems, e.g., involving division remainders, bigger numbers, negative number results, etc., rather than making 100 percent of them simple (C). They should also ask young children guiding questions (the Socratic method) to help them solve problems themselves, rather than just telling them an answer (D).

**40. D:** Experts recommend asking children "why?" questions; *not* expecting certain answers (A) but being open to whatever ideas they may produce; *not* asking questions without permitting or attending to children's answers (B); allowing children enough time to think about what their answers might be rather than demanding immediate responses (C); and listening attentively to the original, sometimes unique, answers that the children come up with on their own by thinking through the questions. This supports children in developing their reasoning skills, which are vital to problem solving, math, and science.

**41. B:** One common event when children begin school is that, through formal math lessons, they view academic math as a group of rules and steps to follow rather than a body of knowledge they can apply to solve real-life problems. Children *do* mathematical thinking before school (A); it is just intuitive rather than formal mathematical thought. As evidenced by the accuracy of (B), children will *not* automatically apply their formal math learning to useful solutions in real life (C); however, teachers can help them learn to do this. One way they can facilitate this transition and application is to provide children with familiar concrete objects that they can manipulate during math lessons, which makes them *more,* not less (D) likely to see connections between math and real life.

**42. C:** Parents and other adults can best help children understand math concepts and procedures by helping them realize how these are applied in many different activities, including other academic subjects like the sciences, arts, and music and a variety of everyday life activities. They should NOT isolate math from life and other school subjects (A). They should NOT just let children do whatever they please and hope that they apply math in these activities (B); instead, they can engage them in activities applying math concepts, like sorting when putting away groceries or setting the table. They should not restrict working on math comprehension to formal math lessons (D), but seek and find math concepts and practices in everyday life routines and events. This will help them understand math better, as well as apply it in practical ways.

**43. A:** One of the earliest evidences of children's developing the idea of symbolic representation— i.e., the concept that things like numbers, letters, words, and objects can be used to represent other things—is their engaging in make-believe and pretend play (e.g., a toy horse represents a real horse; a block is used to represent a cell phone; a stick becomes a laser sword, etc.). Children develop this ability long before they develop fully abstract thought (B). Make-believe and pretend play develop *sooner than* reading, writing, and the alphabetic principle (C), which also employs the concept of symbolic representation. Another example that young children *have* developed symbolic representation is their counting on their fingers (D).

**44. A:** When the teacher supplies the student with the formal math vocabulary word "classifying", s/he is emphasizing the connection of the child's informal math activity of sorting rocks with the formal math vocabulary word that describes it. Asking the child how s/he is sorting the rocks (B) is a better example of the teacher's emphasizing math communication than vocabulary (by having the child explain). Asking, after the child finishes sorting rocks, what other ways s/he could sort them (C) is a better example of emphasizing problem-solving skills than math vocabulary. Therefore (D) is incorrect.

**45. D:** Being aware that patterns (regular repetitions) and relationships (associations between/among things) exist in the world affords us greater self-efficacy about our interacting with the environment, as well as increasing our sense of confidence in the environment itself (C). This awareness not only helps us to understand sequences of events; it moreover enables us to predict the next event in the series before it occurs (B). Having an awareness of patterns and relationships in things also informs our understanding of the basic structure of those things (A).

**46. D:** Commutative. The property that states that the order in which numbers are added does not change the answer is called the commutative property.

**47. C:** Normally developing young children typically learn to count before they have learned the names of all of the numbers. They do NOT typically learn all number names before learning to count (A). They do NOT typically acquire both skills at the same time (B). And they do NOT typically vary individually in the order (D) of acquiring these skills.

**48. B:** When young children have learned how to count, have become familiar with numbers, and have developed good number sense, these three achievements will enable them to add and subtract numbers—i.e., to do beginning arithmetic computations. Children with developed number sense are able to count both forward *and* backward (A). They can also break numbers down into their components, *and* reassemble them (C). Being able to identify relationships between or among numbers *is* an ability that is included in number sense (D).

**49. A:** Bar graph. A bar graph is used to compare quantities. A circle is used to compare parts of a whole. A pictograph shows comparison of quantities using symbols. A line graph shows trends over a period of time.

**50. A:** Young children need concrete objects to manipulate to learn geometry concepts. In early childhood, they think concretely and thus need to see, touch, and manipulate real things to help them understand abstract concepts. Therefore, their memorizing theorems (B) at this age, when most children cannot even read let alone understand them, would be ineffective. Children should be given everyday life activities that teach geometric concepts—e.g., cutting their sandwiches into different geometric shapes, naming these for them, and letting them assemble and/or rearrange the pieces—*before* rather than after (C) they learn formal geometry basics, as activities that are part of daily life are relevant to young children and an effective way to teach concepts. Instructions to draw geometric diagrams (D) are more appropriate when children are older and have learned geometry concepts from interacting with solid objects, and also have better-developed fine motor skills. Certainly adults can help them draw shapes, but this should not be a first and/or isolated exercise.

**51. B:** Measurement is not only a formal system for quantifying amounts and numbers that specify sizes, times, weights, etc. (A). It is also used informally in everyday life. As such, it is a valuable skill that young children can use to recognize and find relationships among real-world objects, outside of academic exercises. Young children are not restricted to standardized rulers, scales, clocks, calendars, etc. (C). They also practice measuring things using whatever is available, e.g., comparing objects to the length of their fingers, hands, feet, etc., or to pieces of string; comparing the heft of an object to that of a block or other toy for weight; comparing how long someone is gone to the duration of a TV show, etc. Measuring practice *does* help children learn to compare object sizes/weights and time periods (D).

**52. C:** Adults can help young children understand the concepts that time passes and is counted and measured by engaging them in counting activities, getting them used to counting in general, telling them how much time various activities took, and showing them the second hand on a clock or watch and counting "One second, two seconds, three…." Young children typically have NOT yet developed understanding of the abstract concept of time (A). However, adults *should* refer to time periods with young children, even before they understand these (B). For example, they can tell children, "You may play for five more minutes before bedtime." Making such references will aid young children's eventual realization of the passage of time. But young children will typically *not* understand such abstract concepts as yesterday/today/tomorrow (D); adults can use more concrete referents, e.g., "after supper" or "before bedtime" until children are older.

**53. D:** To understand fractions, children must know all of these things: what makes up a particular whole unit; how many pieces that unit is divided into; and whether the pieces are all of the same size or not. Knowing the number of parts but not what makes up the unit (A); knowing what comprises the whole unit, but not how many pieces into which it has been divided (B); or knowing both what makes up the whole unit and how many pieces it has been divided into, but not knowing whether the pieces are equal in size or not (C) will not allow children to comprehend the concept of fractions. For example, a child will not understand the idea of thirds if something is divided into three parts of *unequal* size, because each piece is not equal to one-third of the whole.

**54. D:** To be able to make accurate estimates of quantities, children must first understand relative and comparative concepts such as bigger than, smaller than, more of, less of, etc. The process of estimating numbers and amounts in lieu of actual exact measurements helps young children to *learn* math vocabulary words (A) like *around, about, more than, less than,* etc., rather than vice versa. By practicing estimation, children also learn how to make predictions appropriately (B) and attain reasonable estimates (C), rather than the other way around.

**55. D:** Both an insurance company's actuarial table (A) and a weather forecast for the chances of rain (B) predict the probability or likelihood of something happening—for an individual's illness, injury, or death by a given age (A), or for precipitation to occur in a given day or week (B). A chart comparing the results of different interventions (C) organizes and allows people to interpret data related to which method was more or less effective with certain populations rather than predicting the likelihood of any occurrence.

**56. C:** By having each child select his/her favorite star color, the teacher is giving the children experience with collecting things the way adults collect data (i.e., pieces of information). By having them place all stars of each color in separate columns, the teacher gives the children experience with organizing the data they have collected. By labeling each column with one color and placing each star in the corresponding color column, the teacher is giving the children experience with displaying the data they have collected and organized. Determining figure properties (A) would be better illustrated by an activity involving differentiating triangles, octagons, circles, etc. Applying formulas to shapes (B) would work better with school-age children; for example, practice in multiplying length by width to find area. Intuitively identifying probability (D) might involve having the children predict how many of them will choose each star color with the example given.

**57. C:** Charlie's response of ten rectangles is correct. The entire figure is itself a rectangle, making one (A). The four squares within it (B) that Billy saw are also rectangles, making the five (D) that Darlene counted. In addition, connected squares create more rectangles: there are three two-square rectangles and two three-square rectangles. Three and two make five more, for a total of ten.

**58. B:** Ordinal numbers do not indicate the quantity of things but rather their order in a series or set, i.e., the rank or position of each member—the first and third tables here. Choice (A) is an example of cardinal numbers, which indicate quantity or how many—here, four years and two years old. Choice (C) is an example of a nominal number, i.e., one that indicates neither rank nor quantity, but rather a number used as a name to identify something—here, the shirt number of a team player (six). Choice (D) is an example of using rational numbers, i.e., divisions/ratios of integers, or more simply, fractions—two-thirds and one-third here.

**59. B:** The most accurate, and therefore the best answer in this case, is to tell the students that only starting the measurement with zero allows the first inch to be included/counted. Telling them this is how the teacher learned to do it (A) or that this is a convention of standard rulers to be followed

(D) do not offer any explanation of the logic behind measurement; moreover, it is not accurate to say this is done merely to conform. It is equally inaccurate to tell young students this is a way to maximize the use of ruler space (C). Such answers fail to address the central concept that measuring quantities does not begin with a pre-existing quantity of 1.

**60. A:** Children develop shape perception in a chronological sequence, rather than all at once (D). At their youngest, children can identify simple shapes by sight. Only once their linguistic and cognitive skills develop further do they learn the words to name these shapes (B). When they reach the third level of shape perception, children no longer rely only on intuition and appearances, but can also analyze shapes (C), so that they can recognize even a triangle, for example, which is crooked, distorted, taller/thinner/wider than usual, by its constant properties (e.g., three sides, which may be of equal or different lengths).

**61. A:** The teacher is engaging the math skills of 1:1 correspondence by directing the children to place one object on each plate. Practice in counting (B) would be engaged more by, for example, asking children when they line up for an activity, "Who is first? Second? Third?" etc., or by asking them to "count off" in line ("One, two, three...."). Recognizing shapes (C) could be engaged by, for example, asking children when they play with blocks what shape each block has. Size comparison (D) could be engaged by asking children which block or other toy is bigger or smaller than another one.

**62. A:** EC teachers can learn much about how young children are learning new mathematical concepts through observing their behaviors (B); but to help them develop math communication, realize the linguistic functions of math, and develop overall literacy, teachers must also elicit spoken expressions from children about their own knowledge and thought processes. They can do this by asking children questions (e.g., "What shape is this? How about this one? How are these shapes different? Why/how do you think they are different?" etc.). They can then use children's responses to elicit additional expressions from them. While teachers can certainly model language use for children (C) in their speech, including conversations, discussions, directions, and lessons, lecturing (C) is not the best method, especially with young children. Assigning writing about math (D) supports children's reading and writing development and supports literacy too, but is not a substitute for questioning and eliciting further responses.

**63. B:** Spatial awareness is a foundation most related to later understanding the mathematical areas of geometry, which deals with shapes, lines, and other forms and their movements, and physics, which deals with the laws of objects in motion, at rest, etc. Arithmetic {(A), (C)} deals with basic numerical computations, and algebra {(A), (D)} deals with sets of numbers and their relationships, including letter symbols, equations, and formulas, as for solving unknown quantities, etc.

**64. C:** Young children's learning to name numbers (A) is comparable to their learning to name alphabet letters. This reflects the understanding that written/printed symbols represent numerical or alphabetic concepts. Learning to count (B) reflects an additional math skill. But neither of these is the same as understanding that symbols also represent concrete objects found in the real world, which constitutes a major cognitive progression. This understanding is demonstrated by young children when they can view a printed/written number and then count out the corresponding number of objects (like pennies). Therefore, (D) is not true.

**65. D:** 9,731,245/42,754,021 is a fraction. Any number that can be written as a ratio or fraction is rational. The value of pi ($\pi$) (A) is an irrational number, as is the square root of 2 ($\sqrt{2}$) (B), because their numbers to the right of the decimal point continue indefinitely without resolution. Therefore, any decimal number (C) is NOT rational; only decimal numbers that end, and thus can be written as fractions or ratios, are rational.

# Social Studies

**66. B:** According to Erikson's theory of psychosocial development, the earliest stage in a child's first year of life is when s/he develops a basic sense of trust or mistrust in parents and the environment. Having their needs met sufficiently and consistently engenders trust, while having needs met inadequately and/or irregularly spawns mistrust. The second stage, in toddlerhood, involves developing a sense of autonomy or independence (A) versus one of shame and self-doubt. According to Piaget's theory of cognitive development, it is during this time period that children also develop an understanding of symbolic representation, evidenced by their engaging in make-believe or pretend play (D). According to Erikson, preschool children aged around three to five years develop a sense of initiative through exploring and exercising power over their environment, or develop a sense of guilt (C) if they garner disapproval for exerting excessive power.

**67. A:** It is true that conflict resolution steps have been taught successfully to children as young as eighteen months. For example, the HighScope EC curriculum, well known for its effectiveness, has sponsored the expert design of a conflict resolution approach for children aged eighteen months to six years. Conflict mediation and resolution have been taught in such settings as daycare centers, Head Start programs, preschools, nursery schools, and kindergartens. Therefore, (C) is not true. Instruction features the same steps used with adults, but adjusted commensurately with various EC developmental levels. Preschoolers are found to understand these concepts (B) when presented age appropriately. Teaching conflict mediation and resolution to young children is found to develop lifelong social skills and problem-solving skills; hence, children *do* generalize this learning (D).

**68. A:** Authoritative parents are nurturing, responsive, and forgiving; they are assertive but not punitive. They make rules but explain them to children. Authoritarian (B) parents are overly strict, unresponsive, and demanding, and do not explain rules. Permissive (C) parents are nurturing, responsive, and communicative; but are also undemanding, overly indulgent, and avoid discipline. Uninvolved (D) parents are undemanding *and* unresponsive; meeting only basic child needs, they are detached from their children's lives.

**69. B:** Family peacemaker, clown, as well as victim, rescuer, etc., are examples of the family system component of roles. Each member's family role generalizes to school, workplace, and social settings. Boundaries (A) reflect whom and what the family includes or excludes. Rules (C) in families, spoken and unspoken, affect family life in the long term, such as planning ahead to avert problems vs. meeting these as they occur. Equilibrium (D) reflects the consistency and balance in a family.

**70. C:** Collectivist cultures value group harmony and cooperation, while individualist cultures value competition (A), independence (B), and uniqueness (D). World cultures that tend to espouse collectivism include Asian, Latin American, African, and Native American. Those tending to embrace individualism include North American, Canadian, European, and Australian cultures.

**71. D:** Assimilation is the process whereby members of one cultural group (voluntarily or involuntarily) give up their own traditions to adopt those of another culture, often one which is dominant. Acculturation (C) can mean gradual cultural modifications to a person or group through adopting some elements of another culture; the merging of cultures via long-term interaction; or a person's acquiring a society's culture from birth. Accommodation (A) as a general vocabulary word means providing a service (as in hospitality services) or adjustment (as in schools) to meet a need. As a term used by Piaget, it means forming a new schema (concept) or altering an existing one to include new input. Piaget also used assimilation (D) to mean fitting new input into an existing schema without changing the schema. Adaptation (B) in general vocabulary means adjustment; for Piaget, it meant the learning process of assimilation and accommodation combined.

**72. D:** Experts find that cultural competence in educational professionals is not achieved simply by hiring foreign language interpreters and translators (A), or only by hiring racially diverse personnel (B), or just by hiring educators with high self-awareness of their own cultural values (C). Rather, schools must do all three of these things; plus, the educators hired must have and/or develop the communication skills to be able to deliver effective educational services to culturally diverse children and their families, and to conduct meaningful, mutually beneficial interactions and relationships with them.

**73. C:** Researchers in California found that the majority of Latino parents believed their children's capacity for learning was set at birth and would not change, but that only a small minority of White parents held this belief. Hence choices (A) and (B) are incorrect. More White parents are likely to embrace transactional models of child development, seeing their children's learning as a dynamic process involving complex interactions between child and environment. This view is conducive to valuing early childhood stimulation to enhance normal learning, and early intervention to remediate developmental delays. However, the view that a child's cognitive capacity is fixed is conducive to seeing less or no benefit in early stimulation and/or intervention rather than valuing these (D), and hence to not pursuing them.

**74. B:** Various cultures, including African-American as an example, have strong oral traditions. Educators must take this into account rather than focusing on their not reading to their children, or reading to them less often. Telling stories and singing songs is an oral version of developing children's language skills (though it does not confer the same benefits for reading and writing language). Educators must also consider that parents who were not read to themselves as children, and grew up to succeed regardless, are unlikely to value reading to their own children (A). Educators must realize they are unlikely to influence parents whose culture does not value or prioritize reading to children (C). Educators are also unlikely to be able to teach parents to read to their children when the parents do not view children's school readiness and success as benefits of reading to them (D).

**75. A:** Researchers have found that parents from diverse cultures in America vary in their age expectations for many different EC developmental milestones—not just for sleeping alone (B). For instance, Anglo, Filipino, and Puerto Rican parents in the U.S. vary in the ages when they expect their children to eat solid food (C). They also have different ages when they expect their children to sleep through the night (D).

**76. A:** In geography, location—specifically, relative location—determines things like land prices based on the characteristics of an area, which are affected by nearby regions. An example of distance (B) is that land that is close to major highways is more expensive, while land far from main thoroughfares costs less. One example of pattern (C) in geography is that where rock folds form mountains (fold regions), the rivers accordingly form trellis patterns. Another example of pattern, in geographically oriented human behavior, is that settlements in mountainous areas form mainly spreading patterns. An example of interaction (D) in geography is when an industrial city needs raw materials from a rural village for production, and the village needs the city both as a market to buy its resources and for its industrial products: their mutual interdependence creates interaction between them.

**77. B:** Latitudes are lines that run east and west on geographical maps, and are also called parallels. Longitudes (A) are lines that run north and south, so longitude is not a synonym for latitude. Longitudes are also called meridians (C), so meridian is a synonym for longitude, not latitude. Coordinates (D) are the numbers of degrees assigned to various latitudes and latitudes.

**78. C:** A line graph makes clearest how quantities vary across periods of time, by drawing a line connecting each data point so we can see how many/much of something there was each second, minute, hour, day, week, month, year, etc. A pie chart (A) is excellent for clearly visualizing different percentages or proportions, by dividing a "pie" (circle) into "slices" representing what part of the whole each amount represents; however, pie charts do not show change across time the way line graphs do. But a bar graph (B) *can* compare quantities over time; for example, each bar could show the amount of rainfall in a given month. A column of numbers (D) is not a type of graph, and it does not make patterns and trends as clear visually as graphs do.

**79. D:** Teachers can use not only history books (A); they can also assign students to read well-constructed and well-written biographies (B) of famous figures in history and works of historical literature (C), which set even fictionalized stories within real historical periods and events. Historical narratives written in "storytelling" style are also good for engaging student attention while establishing chronological sequences in history.

**80. C:** To help young children understand citizenship concepts, teachers should help them understand the purposes and functions of laws and rules. Understanding these will help them realize that our government is made up of individuals and groups who create and enforce laws. Teachers should also help young children understand that laws limit the powers of authorities (A), preventing them from abusing their roles. Teachers should explain that laws determine the responsibilities of individual citizens (B) like themselves and their family members. They should also point out to young children that laws and rules help to make life and society more predictable, secure, and orderly (D).

## Science

**81. B:** When young children pour sand, water, rice, etc., from one container to another, differently sized (or shaped) container, they are developing basic measurement concepts. Children fitting pegs into matching holes (A) are developing basic 1:1 correspondence concepts. Seeing how many coins they have put into their piggy bank (C) helps children develop basic counting concepts. Separating toys into piles according to type (D), color, shape, size, or any other characteristic helps children develop basic classification/categorization concepts.

**82. A:** When young children learn basic science concepts, an informal learning experience is defined as one wherein the child has choice and control over the activity, but at some point during the activity an adult provides some kind of intervention. When the child has complete choice and control of the activity and no adult intervenes at all (B), this is the definition of a naturalistic learning experience. If the child's activity is chosen and directed by an adult (C), or assigned to a group of children in preschool by the teacher (D), these are examples of structured learning experiences.

**83. B:** When scientists and students are able to identify patterns and find meaning in the results of their experiments, they are using the process skill of Inference. When they use the results of their experiments to formulate new hypotheses (A), they are using the process skill of Prediction. When they identify the properties of objects or situations using their senses, they are using the process skill of Observation. When they report the results of their experiments and their conclusions based [object Object]<br>

<br>

on these results to others (D), they are using the process skill of Communication. These skills are required for solving both math and science problems.

**84. C:** Ammonia is known as a compound gas because its molecules contain atoms of more than one of the chemical elements—nitrogen (B) and hydrogen (D) atoms in the case of ammonia gas. Oxygen (A) as well as nitrogen and hydrogen are elementary gases rather than compound gases because their molecules contain only one chemical element.

**85. D:** Refraction is the process whereby the speed of light is changed as it passes from one transparent medium, like air, to another, like water. The change in speed bends the light wave. Scattering (A) is the process whereby light bounces back at multiple angles when it strikes a rough or uneven surface (instead of bouncing back at a single angle as when it strikes a smooth surface). When light bounces back off a surface, this is reflection (C). Materials that do not reflect *any* light waves (smoothly or scattered) or refract any light waves appear opaque, i.e., we cannot see through them, because they take in all frequencies of light; this is absorption (B).

**86. C:** Magnets do not have to be touching to attract or repel materials; they are able to do this from a distance. However, magnets do NOT work beyond their magnetic fields (D): the magnetic field is defined as the effective range or area of a magnet, so magnets only work within their magnetic fields by definition. Opposite poles of magnets do NOT repel (A), but instead attract each other. Conversely, the like poles of magnets do NOT attract (B), but instead repel one another.

**87. A:** Three ways of transmitting heat are conduction (A), convection (B), and radiation (C). When heat is transmitted through solids, this is done via conduction. Conduction occurs between solid materials directly contacting one another. Convection (B) is how heat travels through liquids and gases. Heat makes them expand, lowering their density so they rise. When they cool, they recover density and fall. This heating-rising and cooling-falling process creates a current known as convection. Radiation (C), like the heat from the sun, occurs when electromagnetic waves travel through space and transfer heat to objects, like the Earth, that they touch. Therefore, (D) is incorrect.

**88. B:** Newton's First Law of Motion states *both* that an object at rest tends to stay at rest (A), and an object in motion tends to stay in motion (C), unless or until an opposing force changes this. Newton's *Third* Law of Motion states that for every action there is an equal and opposite reaction (D).

**89. D:** Sound waves require a physical medium to travel through. This can be a solid, liquid, or gas, but cannot be a vacuum, which is defined as a space lacking matter.

**90. D:** Sedimentary rock is formed on the surface of the earth, deposited in layers as the result of natural processes like erosion. Igneous (A) rocks are formed from volcanic eruptions. Obsidian (B) is just one type of igneous rock. Metamorphic (C) rocks form deep in the earth's crust through heavy pressure and/or heat, which metamorphose or change sedimentary and igneous rocks far below the surface.

**91. C:** Plants growing on land depend on sunlight to perform photosynthesis, the process whereby they convert sunlight's energy to chemical energy as fuel for their life functions. Undersea plants (A) need water and nutrients like land plants; they do not need all gases in the atmosphere but need the gases in the water, and they need less light than land plants, or no light at all, to survive. Mammals (B) need air, water, and nutrients; some mammals need more or less light, but none need light for photosynthesis as land plants do. Humans (D) are also mammals.

**92. D:** Human beings, like other mammals, birds, fish, reptiles, and spiders, have simple life cycles in that they are either born live or hatched from eggs, and then grow to adulthood. Frogs (A), newts (B), and grasshoppers (C) undergo metamorphoses wherein their forms change. Frogs and newts are amphibians; they begin life underwater, breathing through gills, but breathe through lungs by adulthood and move from the water to live on the land. Grasshoppers hatch from eggs into larvae, wormlike juvenile forms that do most of the feeding they need; then they progress to adulthood.

**93. B:** Butterflies undergo a *complete* metamorphosis during their life cycle, i.e., they completely change in form. The stages of a complete metamorphosis are (1) egg, (2) larva, (3) pupa, and (4) imago. Mosquitos (A), dragonflies (C), and grasshoppers (D) all go through an *incomplete* metamorphosis in their life cycles, including the egg, larva, and imago (adult) stages, but not the pupa stage. The butterfly pupa, called a chrysalis, is protected by a cocoon, does not feed, and is inactive until the imago (adult) emerges.

# Health and Physical Education

**94. A:** The U.S. Dept. of HHS targets obesity and tobacco use as the most preventable causes of disability and death. Alcohol use {(B), (C)} also causes disability and death but is not one of HHS' targets in the prevention initiative. (Perhaps HHS officials regard alcohol abuse as not as readily preventable.) Drug abuse (C) is also not a target of this initiative. Diabetes (D) causes disability and death; however, type 1 diabetes is genetic or organic, while type 2 diabetes is largely caused by obesity, which is a target.

**95. B:** Children are liable to be more vulnerable to environmental health risks than adults for several reasons. For one, children's body systems are immature and are still developing, making them easier to damage than those of adults, not vice versa (A). For another, children have smaller body sizes than adults do, so they take in more not fewer (C) toxins through the air they breathe, the water they drink, and the foods they eat. Additionally, the normal behaviors of children expose them to more, not fewer (D) toxins than normal adult behaviors do. Children are more likely to handle and mouth unsanitary and toxic substances and objects; to engage in physical contact with others having contagious illnesses; to go without washing their hands before and after using the bathroom, eating, etc.; to expose themselves unwittingly to various environmental toxins; and to lack experience and judgment about exposure.

**96. C:** The human skin regulates the body's temperature, and the skin is a part of the integumentary systems, which also includes the hair, nails, and sweat and oil glands. The lymphatic (A) system defends the body against infections and helps the circulatory system by returning fluids to the bloodstream. The circulatory (B) system supplies oxygen and nutrients in blood to all body tissue cells, exchanges oxygenated blood for metabolic waste products, and transports waste for elimination. The musculoskeletal (D) system provides body shape, support, stability, and locomotion, and protects the internal organs via bones and muscles. Bones also store minerals, including calcium, and the bone marrow produces blood cells.

**97. D:** The lymphatic system is responsible for producing white blood cells, also known as leukocytes. The lymphatic system is a major part of the immune system, and it also relies on the circulatory system for some functions, such as moving contamination and lymph in the blood. The circulatory system is responsible for pumping blood and nutrients throughout the body. The integumentary system refers to the skin and other external features of the body. The nervous system connects the brain with the muscles and senses, and is responsible for many bodily functions, but is unrelated to the white blood cells.

**98. A:** Cephalocaudal means literally head-to-tail. This is the pattern of physical development for human embryos, fetuses, infants, and children. Proximodistal (B) means development from the inside out, which is also a pattern of human physical growth. (These two are not mutually exclusive but concurrent.) Mediolateral (C) is not a term generally used; but *medial* means toward the midline or closer to the inside, and *lateral* means away from the midline or closer to the outside, so "mediolateral" would have a meaning similar to proximodistal. Intellectual development (D) is like cognitive development and does not refer to patterns of motor or physical development.

**99. B:** When children respond to the challenges of developing increasing levels of control, coordination, speed, strength, agility, and flexibility, and achieve success, this improves their sense of self-efficacy, i.e., of how competent they are to perform and succeed at specific tasks. Children's motor skills generally develop *earlier,* not later than their language skills (A). For this reason, physical activity can offer young children a means of directly expressing themselves as much as arts activities, and before they have developed the language skills to do so (D). Physical activity develops both physical *and* cognitive skills (C) as it requires children to develop closer, more complex coordination of their mental and physical processes, as well as to develop decision-making, problem-solving, judgment, and other cognitive skills.

**100. C:** The NASPE's national standards for physical education include both understanding the main concepts, principles, methods, and techniques of movement and also engaging regularly in physical activity. Hence they do not exclude concepts (A). In addition to engaging in physical activity, these standards also include that an individual be able to demonstrate the motor skills (B) required for doing so. As well as valuing the physical and personal benefits of exercising, these standards moreover do include seeing value in the social benefits of physical activity (D), such as the opportunities that it offers for engaging in social interactions.

**101. C:** The WHO's recommendations include a *minimum* of one hour a day of moderate to vigorous physical activity for children aged five to seventeen. Therefore, a healthy youngster who engages in 15 (A) or 30 (B) minutes per day, or one hour per week (D), of physical activity does not come close to meeting this criterion. However, the recommendation also states that children can engage in either one hour of continuous physical activity, or in shorter, separate increments at different times during the day that add up to a total of one hour.

## Creative and Performing Arts

**102. B:** EC teachers are advised to teach art not only in isolated lessons (A), but moreover to integrate art into the entire curriculum, which is now included in many state standards (C) for early learning and is found to improve children's understanding of many concepts and enhance their learning. Such state standards recommend integrating art projects into both individual learning units and entire curricula (C). When EC teacher assign process activities in art, they should always provide the children in advance with rules and steps (D) for proceeding, and also explain these to the children beforehand.

**103. A:** In addition to integrating art into the science unit and the curriculum, this activity applies artwork to build children's language skills by having them illustrate plants or animals whose names and characteristics they have learned in words; it also builds their vocabularies by having them both represent the word names and concepts of plants or animals visually, and label their pictures with the correct word names. Activities like correctly identifying, comparing, and contrasting word names for different colors of paints, paper, and other art materials are examples of (B). Activities wherein children explore basic visual art elements by viewing and discussing artworks, and experimenting with creating their own lines, shapes, colors, and textures, are examples of (C).

106

Activities wherein teachers ask children to make artworks showing how they feel, representing an idea, or illustrating a story are examples of (D).

**104. B:** The first thing the EC teacher should do when planning an art activity or project is to define which specific concept s/he wants to teach the children. With this done, the teacher should then decide what objectives s/he should fulfill in planning and implementing the activity/project (D), and identify what learning objectives s/he wants the children to meet when they participate in the activity (C). After determining these things, the teacher should then construct a simple product prototype (A). This gives the teacher an idea of the time it will take the children to make a similar product, and facilitates the teacher's determining the best order in which to sequence the activity's steps for the children.

**105. C:** The function of a piece of art is not unrelated to or separate from its context (A); it is necessary to know its context to determine what an artwork's function is. Context is half artist, i.e., his/her historical era, country, and social and political settings inform viewer inferences about the artist's ideas and intentions; and half viewer, i.e., what the art means to the individual viewer in his/her own time period, location, and setting informs his/her perception of and response to the work. Hence context is not dependent solely on one (B) or the other (D).

**106. A:** As students engage in the artistic process of Creating, the teacher's introduction of other students' artworks facilitates their generalizing or transferring what they have learned about this process to the artistic process of Responding when they experience others' creations. (B) has this backward. The Analysis process involves understanding the individual components of an artwork, and seeing how they come together to appreciate the work as a whole (C); the Interpretation {(C), (D)} process involves constructing meaning from experiencing the art. The Evaluation process (D) involves assessing the quality of an artwork.

**107. B:** Yellow is one of the three primary colors. Primary means the color cannot be broken down into any other color, and cannot be produced by mixing other colors. Yellow, red, and blue are the primary colors. Orange (A) is a secondary color, created by mixing the primary colors yellow and red. Green (C) is a secondary color, made by mixing the primary colors blue and yellow. The secondary color purple (D) is produced by mixing the primary colors blue and red.

**108. C:** Pitch is the musical term meaning the frequency of the sound wave of a given musical note. Tempo (A) is the musical term meaning the relative speed of a piece of music, i.e., how slowly or quickly it should be played. Melody (B) is a tune, which is made up of a series of different pitches. Rhythm (D) is both the overall time signature of a musical piece, i.e., how many beats each measure contains, and also the patterns created by varying and repeating the durations of individual notes.

**109. D:** The 3/4 time signature means that there are three beats to each measure, and the quarter note equals one beat. A way to make 3/4 or waltz time easy to hear is to count, "*One* two three, *one* two three" repeatedly, stressing the first beat. 2/2 (A), or cut time, means there are two beats to each measure and the half note equals one beat. In 2/4 (B) time, there are two beats to every measure and the quarter note equals one beat. In 4/4 (C) time, there are four beats to a measure and the quarter note equals one beat. Waltz time has three counts per measure, rather than an even number (2 or 4) like the others.

**110. B:** While Beethoven's work included all of these organizing principles, as well as balance and unity (as great works of art generally do), the principle related specifically to its very famous and familiar main theme is repetition. The composer begins the symphony with this four-note theme and repeats it throughout—the same way, plus transposing it to different notes with the same intervals and rhythm, etc., creating striking and memorable effects while reinforcing the piece's structure.

# General Pedagogy

**111. C:** The libido is part of the id according to Freud. It represents psychic energy as well as sex drive. Freud's three major personality structures are the id (A), which generates unconscious impulses; the ego (B), which realistically regulates acting on id impulses; and the superego (C), which morally regulates the id and ego.

**112. B:** Schemata (plural of schema) are mental constructs or concepts of categories or classes of things, e.g. things I can suck on; things I can throw; furry four-legged animals, etc. They are not concepts of individual objects (A). They are not programs only for motor actions (C), but ideas for categorizing different components of the environment. Inborn reflexes are not governed by ideas (D) but are automatic reactions.

**113. A:** Elements of critical thinking include distinguishing fact from opinion (C) in text or speech by looking for objectivity, facts, and proof vs. subjectivity, non-factual information, and absence of proof; finding evidence or no evidence (D) to support the writer or speaker's arguments by examining the text or speech; evaluating evidence used to support (A) arguments or statements by considering whether its source is reputable, proven, and accepted by authorities in the field; and judging the quality of material (B) or information by comparing it to other material/information, consulting one's own previous experience, and listening to one's own intuition.

**114. D:** Psychologists studying infant behaviors have classified their basic temperaments into Easy, Difficult, and Slow to Warm Up. They find that the majority of babies have the Easy temperament. Thus (A) is incorrect, and babies with Difficult temperaments are not in the majority (B); neither are Slow to Warm Up types (C).

**115. C:** One of the characteristics Adler described about the youngest siblings in families is that being the smallest, they often wish to be bigger than their older siblings; so as they grow, they may make grandiose plans which never succeed. Adler found that while youngest children, unlike only children, have multiple older siblings who "parent" them, they also have in common with only children (A) the fact that they are never displaced ("dethroned") by younger siblings. Adler observed that one twin is usually more active or stronger than the other and perceived by parents as older; and that the twin born a minute or more earlier may be perceived by the parents as more mature (B). Adler noted that one twin may develop a leadership role while the other may develop identity issues (D). Adler also commented that while some "babies" of the family may grow out of this role, others continue to feel and behave as the baby of the family indefinitely.

**116. B:** Maslow conceived of human needs in a hierarchy, and visualized this hierarchy as a pyramid. At the base of this pyramid are physiological needs, which are the most fundamental. Above these are security (C) needs such as shelter and a safe environment. Above these are social needs like feeling loved and belonging to a group. Above these are esteem (D) needs like feeling personal value, social recognition, and accomplishment. At the top of the pyramid are self-actualizing (A) needs, i.e. realizing one's full potential and attaining optimal personal growth. Maslow theorized that lower levels of need must be met before any higher level(s) can be addressed; hence physiological needs must be met first.

**117. C:** Conditional positive self-regard was Rogers' term for self-esteem that depends on external standards. External locus of control was Julian Rotter's term for attributing one's own success or

failure to external factors (e.g. "The teacher didn't explain it to me" for failure or "The teacher helped me" for success). Conditional positive self-regard would be the equivalent in Rogers' theory. Rogers felt that children develop conditional positive self-regard when they are subjected to condition of worth (B), i.e. rewards based not on need but worthiness, as in behaviorism's contingencies of reinforcement. Rogers believed Incongruence (A) between one's ideal self and real self would cause neurosis. Unconditional positive regard (D) was what Rogers believed parents and therapists should give, i.e. unconditional love and acceptance, to children and all individuals.

**118. C:** EC experts say that indoor learning environments for toddlers and preschoolers should have the rooms organized to enable a variety of activities, but not necessarily to limit the activities to certain areas (A). The floors in the rooms should include both hard and carpeted floors (B) to allow crawling, toddling, walking, etc., which should not be limited by insufficient space. Preschool math and science activities might occur in multiple areas of a classroom (D), while the room still should be laid out to facilitate their taking place.

**119. C:** Positive reinforcement (A) motivates the individuals by presenting something that increases the probability of a behavior's occurrence and/or recurrence. Primary reinforcement (B) is unconditioned, i.e., it naturally reinforces or increases a behavior's probability (e.g., food, water, sleep). Negative reinforcement (C) motivates the individuals by removing something whose removal reinforces or increases a behavior's probability. Secondary reinforcement (D) is conditioned, i.e., it did not originally reinforce the behavior but has been made to do so by pairing it with a primary reinforcement.

**120. D:** Small inner rooms and partitions in indoor environments provide ways for children to experience privacy and solitude when needed. Adult laps for cuddling (A), pillows and soft upholstery (B) and thickly carpeted floor areas (C) are all related to providing for children's sensory needs for softness, but not for privacy.

# How to Overcome Test Anxiety

Just the thought of taking a test is enough to make most people a little nervous. A test is an important event that can have a long-term impact on your future, so it's important to take it seriously and it's natural to feel anxious about performing well. But just because anxiety is normal, that doesn't mean that it's helpful in test taking, or that you should simply accept it as part of your life. Anxiety can have a variety of effects. These effects can be mild, like making you feel slightly nervous, or severe, like blocking your ability to focus or remember even a simple detail.

If you experience test anxiety—whether severe or mild—it's important to know how to beat it. To discover this, first you need to understand what causes test anxiety.

## Causes of Test Anxiety

While we often think of anxiety as an uncontrollable emotional state, it can actually be caused by simple, practical things. One of the most common causes of test anxiety is that a person does not feel adequately prepared for their test. This feeling can be the result of many different issues such as poor study habits or lack of organization, but the most common culprit is time management. Starting to study too late, failing to organize your study time to cover all of the material, or being distracted while you study will mean that you're not well prepared for the test. This may lead to cramming the night before, which will cause you to be physically and mentally exhausted for the test. Poor time management also contributes to feelings of stress, fear, and hopelessness as you realize you are not well prepared but don't know what to do about it.

Other times, test anxiety is not related to your preparation for the test but comes from unresolved fear. This may be a past failure on a test, or poor performance on tests in general. It may come from comparing yourself to others who seem to be performing better or from the stress of living up to expectations. Anxiety may be driven by fears of the future—how failure on this test would affect your educational and career goals. These fears are often completely irrational, but they can still negatively impact your test performance.

> **Review Video: 3 Reasons You Have Test Anxiety**
> Visit mometrix.com/academy and enter code: 428468

## Elements of Test Anxiety

As mentioned earlier, test anxiety is considered to be an emotional state, but it has physical and mental components as well. Sometimes you may not even realize that you are suffering from test anxiety until you notice the physical symptoms. These can include trembling hands, rapid heartbeat, sweating, nausea, and tense muscles. Extreme anxiety may lead to fainting or vomiting. Obviously, any of these symptoms can have a negative impact on testing. It is important to recognize them as soon as they begin to occur so that you can address the problem before it damages your performance.

> **Review Video: 3 Ways to Tell You Have Test Anxiety**
> Visit mometrix.com/academy and enter code: 927847

The mental components of test anxiety include trouble focusing and inability to remember learned information. During a test, your mind is on high alert, which can help you recall information and stay focused for an extended period of time. However, anxiety interferes with your mind's natural processes, causing you to blank out, even on the questions you know well. The strain of testing during anxiety makes it difficult to stay focused, especially on a test that may take several hours. Extreme anxiety can take a huge mental toll, making it difficult not only to recall test information but even to understand the test questions or pull your thoughts together.

> **Review Video: How Test Anxiety Affects Memory**
> Visit mometrix.com/academy and enter code: 609003

## Effects of Test Anxiety

Test anxiety is like a disease—if left untreated, it will get progressively worse. Anxiety leads to poor performance, and this reinforces the feelings of fear and failure, which in turn lead to poor performances on subsequent tests. It can grow from a mild nervousness to a crippling condition. If allowed to progress, test anxiety can have a big impact on your schooling, and consequently on your future.

Test anxiety can spread to other parts of your life. Anxiety on tests can become anxiety in any stressful situation, and blanking on a test can turn into panicking in a job situation. But fortunately, you don't have to let anxiety rule your testing and determine your grades. There are a number of relatively simple steps you can take to move past anxiety and function normally on a test and in the rest of life.

> **Review Video: How Test Anxiety Impacts Your Grades**
> Visit mometrix.com/academy and enter code: 939819

# Physical Steps for Beating Test Anxiety

While test anxiety is a serious problem, the good news is that it can be overcome. It doesn't have to control your ability to think and remember information. While it may take time, you can begin taking steps today to beat anxiety.

Just as your first hint that you may be struggling with anxiety comes from the physical symptoms, the first step to treating it is also physical. Rest is crucial for having a clear, strong mind. If you are tired, it is much easier to give in to anxiety. But if you establish good sleep habits, your body and mind will be ready to perform optimally, without the strain of exhaustion. Additionally, sleeping well helps you to retain information better, so you're more likely to recall the answers when you see the test questions.

Getting good sleep means more than going to bed on time. It's important to allow your brain time to relax. Take study breaks from time to time so it doesn't get overworked, and don't study right before bed. Take time to rest your mind before trying to rest your body, or you may find it difficult to fall asleep.

> **Review Video: <u>The Importance of Sleep for Your Brain</u>**
> Visit mometrix.com/academy and enter code: 319338

Along with sleep, other aspects of physical health are important in preparing for a test. Good nutrition is vital for good brain function. Sugary foods and drinks may give a burst of energy but this burst is followed by a crash, both physically and emotionally. Instead, fuel your body with protein and vitamin-rich foods.

Also, drink plenty of water. Dehydration can lead to headaches and exhaustion, especially if your brain is already under stress from the rigors of the test. Particularly if your test is a long one, drink water during the breaks. And if possible, take an energy-boosting snack to eat between sections.

> **Review Video: <u>How Diet Can Affect your Mood</u>**
> Visit mometrix.com/academy and enter code: 624317

Along with sleep and diet, a third important part of physical health is exercise. Maintaining a steady workout schedule is helpful, but even taking 5-minute study breaks to walk can help get your blood pumping faster and clear your head. Exercise also releases endorphins, which contribute to a positive feeling and can help combat test anxiety.

When you nurture your physical health, you are also contributing to your mental health. If your body is healthy, your mind is much more likely to be healthy as well. So take time to rest, nourish your body with healthy food and water, and get moving as much as possible. Taking these physical steps will make you stronger and more able to take the mental steps necessary to overcome test anxiety.

> **Review Video: <u>How to Stay Healthy and Prevent Test Anxiety</u>**
> Visit mometrix.com/academy and enter code: 877894

# Mental Steps for Beating Test Anxiety

Working on the mental side of test anxiety can be more challenging, but as with the physical side, there are clear steps you can take to overcome it. As mentioned earlier, test anxiety often stems from lack of preparation, so the obvious solution is to prepare for the test. Effective studying may be the most important weapon you have for beating test anxiety, but you can and should employ several other mental tools to combat fear.

First, boost your confidence by reminding yourself of past success—tests or projects that you aced. If you're putting as much effort into preparing for this test as you did for those, there's no reason you should expect to fail here. Work hard to prepare; then trust your preparation.

Second, surround yourself with encouraging people. It can be helpful to find a study group, but be sure that the people you're around will encourage a positive attitude. If you spend time with others who are anxious or cynical, this will only contribute to your own anxiety. Look for others who are motivated to study hard from a desire to succeed, not from a fear of failure.

Third, reward yourself. A test is physically and mentally tiring, even without anxiety, and it can be helpful to have something to look forward to. Plan an activity following the test, regardless of the outcome, such as going to a movie or getting ice cream.

When you are taking the test, if you find yourself beginning to feel anxious, remind yourself that you know the material. Visualize successfully completing the test. Then take a few deep, relaxing breaths and return to it. Work through the questions carefully but with confidence, knowing that you are capable of succeeding.

Developing a healthy mental approach to test taking will also aid in other areas of life. Test anxiety affects more than just the actual test—it can be damaging to your mental health and even contribute to depression. It's important to beat test anxiety before it becomes a problem for more than testing.

**Review Video: Test Anxiety and Depression**
Visit mometrix.com/academy and enter code: 904704

# Study Strategy

Being prepared for the test is necessary to combat anxiety, but what does being prepared look like? You may study for hours on end and still not feel prepared. What you need is a strategy for test prep. The next few pages outline our recommended steps to help you plan out and conquer the challenge of preparation.

## STEP 1: SCOPE OUT THE TEST

Learn everything you can about the format (multiple choice, essay, etc.) and what will be on the test. Gather any study materials, course outlines, or sample exams that may be available. Not only will this help you to prepare, but knowing what to expect can help to alleviate test anxiety.

## STEP 2: MAP OUT THE MATERIAL

Look through the textbook or study guide and make note of how many chapters or sections it has. Then divide these over the time you have. For example, if a book has 15 chapters and you have five days to study, you need to cover three chapters each day. Even better, if you have the time, leave an extra day at the end for overall review after you have gone through the material in depth.

If time is limited, you may need to prioritize the material. Look through it and make note of which sections you think you already have a good grasp on, and which need review. While you are studying, skim quickly through the familiar sections and take more time on the challenging parts. Write out your plan so you don't get lost as you go. Having a written plan also helps you feel more in control of the study, so anxiety is less likely to arise from feeling overwhelmed at the amount to cover.

## STEP 3: GATHER YOUR TOOLS

Decide what study method works best for you. Do you prefer to highlight in the book as you study and then go back over the highlighted portions? Or do you type out notes of the important information? Or is it helpful to make flashcards that you can carry with you? Assemble the pens, index cards, highlighters, post-it notes, and any other materials you may need so you won't be distracted by getting up to find things while you study.

If you're having a hard time retaining the information or organizing your notes, experiment with different methods. For example, try color-coding by subject with colored pens, highlighters, or post-it notes. If you learn better by hearing, try recording yourself reading your notes so you can listen while in the car, working out, or simply sitting at your desk. Ask a friend to quiz you from your flashcards, or try teaching someone the material to solidify it in your mind.

## STEP 4: CREATE YOUR ENVIRONMENT

It's important to avoid distractions while you study. This includes both the obvious distractions like visitors and the subtle distractions like an uncomfortable chair (or a too-comfortable couch that makes you want to fall asleep). Set up the best study environment possible: good lighting and a comfortable work area. If background music helps you focus, you may want to turn it on, but otherwise keep the room quiet. If you are using a computer to take notes, be sure you don't have any other windows open, especially applications like social media, games, or anything else that could distract you. Silence your phone and turn off notifications. Be sure to keep water close by so you stay hydrated while you study (but avoid unhealthy drinks and snacks).

Also, take into account the best time of day to study. Are you freshest first thing in the morning? Try to set aside some time then to work through the material. Is your mind clearer in the afternoon or evening? Schedule your study session then. Another method is to study at the same time of day that you will take the test, so that your brain gets used to working on the material at that time and will be ready to focus at test time.

## STEP 5: STUDY!

Once you have done all the study preparation, it's time to settle into the actual studying. Sit down, take a few moments to settle your mind so you can focus, and begin to follow your study plan. Don't give in to distractions or let yourself procrastinate. This is your time to prepare so you'll be ready to fearlessly approach the test. Make the most of the time and stay focused.

Of course, you don't want to burn out. If you study too long you may find that you're not retaining the information very well. Take regular study breaks. For example, taking five minutes out of every hour to walk briskly, breathing deeply and swinging your arms, can help your mind stay fresh.

As you get to the end of each chapter or section, it's a good idea to do a quick review. Remind yourself of what you learned and work on any difficult parts. When you feel that you've mastered the material, move on to the next part. At the end of your study session, briefly skim through your notes again.

But while review is helpful, cramming last minute is NOT. If at all possible, work ahead so that you won't need to fit all your study into the last day. Cramming overloads your brain with more information than it can process and retain, and your tired mind may struggle to recall even previously learned information when it is overwhelmed with last-minute study. Also, the urgent nature of cramming and the stress placed on your brain contribute to anxiety. You'll be more likely to go to the test feeling unprepared and having trouble thinking clearly.

So don't cram, and don't stay up late before the test, even just to review your notes at a leisurely pace. Your brain needs rest more than it needs to go over the information again. In fact, plan to finish your studies by noon or early afternoon the day before the test. Give your brain the rest of the day to relax or focus on other things, and get a good night's sleep. Then you will be fresh for the test and better able to recall what you've studied.

## STEP 6: TAKE A PRACTICE TEST

Many courses offer sample tests, either online or in the study materials. This is an excellent resource to check whether you have mastered the material, as well as to prepare for the test format and environment.

Check the test format ahead of time: the number of questions, the type (multiple choice, free response, etc.), and the time limit. Then create a plan for working through them. For example, if you have 30 minutes to take a 60-question test, your limit is 30 seconds per question. Spend less time on the questions you know well so that you can take more time on the difficult ones.

If you have time to take several practice tests, take the first one open book, with no time limit. Work through the questions at your own pace and make sure you fully understand them. Gradually work up to taking a test under test conditions: sit at a desk with all study materials put away and set a timer. Pace yourself to make sure you finish the test with time to spare and go back to check your answers if you have time.

After each test, check your answers. On the questions you missed, be sure you understand why you missed them. Did you misread the question (tests can use tricky wording)? Did you forget the information? Or was it something you hadn't learned? Go back and study any shaky areas that the practice tests reveal.

Taking these tests not only helps with your grade, but also aids in combating test anxiety. If you're already used to the test conditions, you're less likely to worry about it, and working through tests until you're scoring well gives you a confidence boost. Go through the practice tests until you feel comfortable, and then you can go into the test knowing that you're ready for it.

## Test Tips

On test day, you should be confident, knowing that you've prepared well and are ready to answer the questions. But aside from preparation, there are several test day strategies you can employ to maximize your performance.

First, as stated before, get a good night's sleep the night before the test (and for several nights before that, if possible). Go into the test with a fresh, alert mind rather than staying up late to study.

Try not to change too much about your normal routine on the day of the test. It's important to eat a nutritious breakfast, but if you normally don't eat breakfast at all, consider eating just a protein bar. If you're a coffee drinker, go ahead and have your normal coffee. Just make sure you time it so that the caffeine doesn't wear off right in the middle of your test. Avoid sugary beverages, and drink enough water to stay hydrated but not so much that you need a restroom break 10 minutes into the test. If your test isn't first thing in the morning, consider going for a walk or doing a light workout before the test to get your blood flowing.

Allow yourself enough time to get ready, and leave for the test with plenty of time to spare so you won't have the anxiety of scrambling to arrive in time. Another reason to be early is to select a good seat. It's helpful to sit away from doors and windows, which can be distracting. Find a good seat, get out your supplies, and settle your mind before the test begins.

When the test begins, start by going over the instructions carefully, even if you already know what to expect. Make sure you avoid any careless mistakes by following the directions.

Then begin working through the questions, pacing yourself as you've practiced. If you're not sure on an answer, don't spend too much time on it, and don't let it shake your confidence. Either skip it and come back later, or eliminate as many wrong answers as possible and guess among the remaining ones. Don't dwell on these questions as you continue—put them out of your mind and focus on what lies ahead.

Be sure to read all of the answer choices, even if you're sure the first one is the right answer. Sometimes you'll find a better one if you keep reading. But don't second-guess yourself if you do immediately know the answer. Your gut instinct is usually right. Don't let test anxiety rob you of the information you know.

If you have time at the end of the test (and if the test format allows), go back and review your answers. Be cautious about changing any, since your first instinct tends to be correct, but make sure you didn't misread any of the questions or accidentally mark the wrong answer choice. Look over any you skipped and make an educated guess.

At the end, leave the test feeling confident. You've done your best, so don't waste time worrying about your performance or wishing you could change anything. Instead, celebrate the successful completion of this test. And finally, use this test to learn how to deal with anxiety even better next time.

> **Review Video: 5 Tips to Beat Test Anxiety**
> Visit mometrix.com/academy and enter code: 570656

## Important Qualification

Not all anxiety is created equal. If your test anxiety is causing major issues in your life beyond the classroom or testing center, or if you are experiencing troubling physical symptoms related to your anxiety, it may be a sign of a serious physiological or psychological condition. If this sounds like your situation, we strongly encourage you to seek professional help.

# Thank You

We at Mometrix would like to extend our heartfelt thanks to you, our friend and patron, for allowing us to play a part in your journey. It is a privilege to serve people from all walks of life who are unified in their commitment to building the best future they can for themselves.

The preparation you devote to these important testing milestones may be the most valuable educational opportunity you have for making a real difference in your life. We encourage you to put your heart into it—that feeling of succeeding, overcoming, and yes, conquering will be well worth the hours you've invested.

We want to hear your story, your struggles and your successes, and if you see any opportunities for us to improve our materials so we can help others even more effectively in the future, please share that with us as well. **The team at Mometrix would be absolutely thrilled to hear from you!** So please, send us an email (support@mometrix.com) and let's stay in touch.

> **If you'd like some additional help, check out these other resources we offer for your exam:**
> **http://MometrixFlashcards.com/PraxisII**

# Additional Bonus Material

Due to our efforts to try to keep this book to a manageable length, we've created a link that will give you access to all of your additional bonus material.

> **Please visit**
> **http://www.mometrix.com/bonus948/priieced5025 to access**
> **the information.**

# IMPROVE YOUR SCORE WITH

# Mometrix®

## PREP THAT EMPOWERS

At Mometrix, we think differently about tests. We believe you can perform better on your exam by implementing a few critical strategies and focusing your study time on what's most important. With so many demands on your time, you probably don't have months to spend preparing for an exam that holds the key to your future. Our team of testing experts devote hours upon hours to painstakingly review piles of content and boil it all down to the critical concepts that are most likely to be on your exam. We do a lot of work cutting through the fluff to give you what you need the most to perform well on the exam. But you don't have to take our word for it; here is what some of our customers have to say:

✓ *"I have just retaken my test and I scored way better than my previous score. I had this program for only 3 days and I just want to say that I can't believe how well it worked." - Mandy C.*

✓ *"Just wanted to say thank you. Due to your product I was able to ace my exam with very little effort. Your tricks did the trick. Thanks again, and I would recommend this product to anyone." - Erich L.*

✓ *"Just dropping you a note to let you know that I am completely satisfied with the product. I had already taken the test once and landed in the 75th percentile of those taking it with me. I took the test a second time and used some of your tips and raised my score to the 97th percentile. Thanks for my much improved score." - Denise W.*

✓ *"I just wanted to tell you I had ordered your study guide, and I finally aced the test after taking it numerous times. I tried tutors and all sorts of study guides and nothing helped. Your guide did the job and got me the score I needed! Thank you!" - Nicholas R.*

## We offer study materials for over 1000 different standardized exams, including:

**Business and Career**
**Construction and Industry**
**Counseling and Social Work**
**Finance, Insurance, and Real Estate**

**Medical and Nursing**
**Teacher Certification**
**K-12**
**College Admissions and Placement**

For questions about bulk discounts or ordering through your company/institution, contact our Institutional Sales Department at 888-248-1219 or sales@mometrix.com.

Visit www.MometrixCatalog.com for our full list of products and services.

Mometrix utilizes a state-of-the-art, European-engineered square-fold mechanical book binding process, which avoids the use of chemical-based glues and minimizes energy consumption in the manufacturing process.

Made in USA

ISBN: 978-1-5167-0317-3

9 781516 703173